GOD GAVE THE WORD

GOD GAVE THE WORD

A Collection of WORD-based Essays, Poems and Songs

Ron Schoolcraft

WOODSONG

God Gave The Word

A Collection of WORD-based Essays, Poems and Songs

Ron Schoolcraft

2024 All rights reserved.

ISBN: 978-1-961482-13-5

Printed in the USA

CONTENTS

TO:

Rhonda and Bryan Bowling

Angela and Scott Marshall

Julia and Kevin Bowling

PREFACE

I still remember my surprise on December 18, 2019, when Senior Sunday School Class leader, Tom Spall, invited me to be one of the six teachers of our class. My immediate response was, "Oh, I think I'm too old, Brother Spall." Just then, one of my favorite teachers, Brother Bernard Gray, a spry ninety years old, brushed past, shouting, "Glory!" as he entered the classroom. Brother Spall didn't have to say a word, his big smile said, "Gotcha!" "But," I tried again. "I'm still a newbie; I'm sure Pastor Arrowood has guidelines about not using new members until they have attended at least a year," I politely opted out. (I had been attending for a year and a half but a member for only about nine months).

"I've already cleared it with him, and he thought it was a great idea," Tom parried with a smile. "He seemed genuinely excited and quickly okayed it." I felt a little unsteady, like someone had just pulled a rug out from under me. Okay, it was time to play my trump card: the real reason for my reluctance. Ever since losing my beloved soulmate, Marcella, on May 10, 2018, my world had literally been turned upside down. I was devastated beyond words and still grieving heavily. I told people, truthfully, she was not just my "better half," but she was my better "three-fourths," at least. And I didn't feel like there was much left of me after she went to her heavenly reward. I was quick to confess that I had been blessed above all to be married to this Proverbs 31 "virtuous woman" for fifty-five glorious years. "Many daughters have done virtuously, but thou [Marcella] excellest them all" (Proverbs 31:29 [Marcella] added). This is how I felt. Still do.

Before I could play my "sympathy" card, I felt a check in my spirit: *You need to do this; it will help you.* "Let me pray about it, Brother Spall, and I'll let you know next week," I said, when I could have and should have said, "Yes!" right then. The next Sunday I said, "Yes." With his trademark grin, he handed me the new teachers' schedule: My name was *already on it*! He already knew! That same day, Kevin Mullen asked me to prepare to give a "presentation" at an upcoming men's session. I said, "Yes, Lord, help me!"

Teaching my first lesson a few weeks later, I told the class I hadn't taught Sunday School since I was in my thirties teaching junior high students. When I asked them if they wouldn't mind pretending to be 7th and 8th graders, they seemed delighted. They've been pretending ever since. A few weeks later, at the conclusion of my second lesson, Sister Bozarth complimented me: "You didn't look nearly as scared as you did the first time. You actually had some color in your face." I began to think I might make it.

Thus began a surprisingly enjoyable four years (and counting) of teaching as I was challenged to draw closer to God in lesson preparation and to try to be a blessing in sharing what the Lord gave me. And so it was, as I was pondering the possibility of sharing with others some of the good things that I felt the Lord had given me (maybe in book format) that Psalm 68:11 leapt out at me: "The Lord gave the word: great was the company of those that published it." There it was: a confirmation that I had not even asked for, and a title for my book — *God Gave the Word.* Both were neatly gift-wrapped in one compelling verse of Scripture! Thank you, Jesus! I did not need the gift of interpretation to know immediately my next stop was Pastor Larry Arrowood and Woodsong Publishing.

Here I must pause to express my deep, heartfelt thanks and sincere appreciation to Woodsong Publishing and Pastor Larry Arrowood, Jaredith Mize, Matthew Arrowood, and Sharon Mize for their invaluable help, assistance, and expertise in publishing *God Gave the Word.* They brought to fruition my desire to: "... publish the name of the LORD: ascribe ye greatness unto our God" (Deuteronomy 32:3).

Pastor Larry Arrowood and Pastor-elect Aaron Arrowood have kept me: "... planted in the house of the LORD ..." that I might "... flourish in the courts of our God. They shall still bring forth fruit in old age; they shall be fat and flourishing" (Psalm 92:13-14)! And I can't thank Brother Tom Spall enough for asking me to teach, then being my mentor and chief encourager. Thank you for minding the Lord!

My sincere prayer is that you, the reader, will be blessed in reading *God Gave the Word* as much as I was in writing it. If you are, then you will be abundantly blessed indeed. And I pray that, as you read, you will realize, "... the word is very nigh unto thee, in thy mouth, and in thy heart, that thou mayest do it" (Deuteronomy 30:14).

"Now unto him that is able to keep you from falling, and to present you faultless before the presence of his glory with exceeding joy, To the only wise God our Saviour, be glory and majesty, dominion and power, both now and ever. Amen" (Jude 24-25)!

PART I

THE WORD

Ten Reasons Why the Bible is God's Word

1. Highly Reasonable and a Necessity

Science has been proving for decades how incredibly complex this creation is, and that the best and only logical explanation for it is that it took a very intelligent, transcendent Creator to bring it into existence. Since it is profoundly clear that a creation demands a Creator, it follows that He would be intelligent enough to design and provide a way to communicate with us. "The delusion that this beautiful, intricately complex cosmos, with its multitude of marvelously designed living creatures, could have evolved itself by chance is absurd in the highest degree!"[1] Our bodies are marvels of engineering design: all the complex systems work together: respiratory, digestive, and circulatory. The blood circulates through the lungs, picks up oxygen, takes the oxygen and food nutrients from the digestive system and distributes them to every cell in the body through arteries, all the blood vessels and small capillaries; further, it picks up the cellular waste products, e.g. CO_2 (carbon dioxide), for the return trip. Then it dumps off the CO_2 in the lungs where it's exhaled. Also, we have the body's amazing defense system and self-healing mechanisms (e.g. blood clots and white blood cells). All these systems had to be created simultaneously or they would not work. They were all created and coordinated simultaneously to work together.

The famous agnostic, Isaac Asimov, said that the three-pound human brain is the most complex and orderly arrangement of matter in the universe! It's much more complex than computers and computer programs made by intelligent men. So, the brain (scientists still don't understand all its mysteries) and the eye—with its millions of cells—all came about by chance? All this intricate design could not come about by chance accidents and mistakes, such as mutations, that are almost always harmful. All this complex design demands a Designer, laws demand a Lawgiver (e.g., the law of gravity, the conservation of energy, the I and II Laws of Thermodynamics); and, again, a creation demands a Creator. Matthew Henry, in his commentary on Genesis said, "Evolutionists are the world's biggest fools. They see a world that couldn't make itself, yet they will not admit that there was a God who made it."[2] The Bible rightly says: "Professing themselves to be wise, they became fools" (Romans 1:22); and, "The fool hath said in his heart, there is no God" (Psalm 14:1).

The amazing DNA is a microscopic molecule that contains the genetic blueprint, or recipe, for life for all living organisms. It contains instructions for the development, functions, growth, and reproduction of genes. DNA is coded in a spiral double helix, with reams of information jam-packed and coded along its spine. "Codes" speak of intelligence and intelligent design. One reason the U.S. and the Allies won WWII was because codebreakers solved the German and Japanese codes. It took great intelligence to create those codes as well as to break them.

Scientists have also discovered that the universe is fine-tuned, and planet earth is uniquely fine-tuned for intelligent life! This fine-tuning of the physical laws and constants requires that they have the precise numerical values to sustain life. Parameters such as the expansion rate of the universe (the cosmological constant), the location of the earth at just the right distance from the sun (a little closer and it would be too hot to sustain life, and a little further away, too cold), the force of gravity, earth's size and atmosphere, and many intricate cycles such as the carbon, oxygen and nitrogen cycles, etc., testify to the degree to which our planet and universe are exquisitely and precariously balanced and fine-tuned! It takes an intelligent mind to produce finely tuned devices, such as space shuttles, computers, microchips, smart phones, the internet, etc. Fine-tuning requires a Fine-tuner!

Anyone who is open-minded and honest must realize that a transcendent God fashioned and fine-tuned this universe and planet earth and placed man on it as the highest form of God's creation! But, why? To what purpose? There must have been a purpose and a plan. So, how can we find out what it is? The loving, transcendent, one true God would surely be responsible and intelligent enough to communicate with us to reveal His divine plan and purpose. But how would He communicate with us? Would He write it across the sky using cloud configurations? How about using the alignment of the stars to spell out what we need to know? Or a stellar broadcast from heaven's website?

What better way than to cause a BOOK to be written? To inspire and breathe upon called and chosen Holy men to write His Book, carefully guiding them and leading them. This super-intelligent Designer, Creator, and Fine-tuner was Omniscient, Omnipotent and Omnipresent enough to bless us with the BOOK OF GOD, the HOLY BIBLE, to have and to hold, to show us the Way, the Truth and the Life. It's His Love Letter to us, His Guidebook, His Manufacturer's Handbook, His Roadmap, Compass, and GPS for us! It contains the unsearchable riches and wisdom of Heaven, the revelation of God in Jesus Christ, inspiration for the soul, and instruction for the mind to reveal the plan of salvation: to reveal that He became one of us, to die for us and redeem us, so that we could be one with Him! And the more we read, the more we become convinced there is a transcendent, controlling MIND behind it!

2. Amazing Composition

The Bible is composed of sixty-six books, written by forty different authors, covering four thousand years of man's history, consuming sixteen hundred years in the writing, in three different languages. In addition, the writers were from many different walks of life: fishermen, farmers, shepherds, military leaders, tentmakers, a doctor, prisoners, governors, kings, and even an IRS man (tax collector, Matthew). Yet, despite all this, **it reads as ONE book**! It seems the watermark of God's wisdom is on every page, and a portrait of Christ is on almost every page! One could not take any other subject, like, for example, science, and try to assemble and collect writings from sixty-six books, by forty authors, written over the last sixteen hundred years, covering four thousand years of history, and have it make any sense. We would get a hodgepodge of contradictions, utter chaos, and a mumble-jumble of laughable, nonsensical meanderings: especially in science, since theories change often.

The Bible has one system of doctrine and one plan of salvation: in the Old Testament, we're looking for the Messiah; in the New Testament, He's Here! One Lord, one faith, one baptism! One amazing book – the composition is utterly unexplainable, except as miraculous and amazing! It's like a symphony orchestra with different sections and instruments. The Composer/Director skillfully arranged every part so it blends and crescendos into a grand finale, with everyone on their feet, a phenomenal work of art — a Masterpiece! No other book reveals the origin of the universe and planet earth, the origin of life, of sin, and of death, showing what has happened to cause sorrow, pain, and death, and a universe and planet earth suffering under the bondage of decay and corruption. And best of all, the Bible is the book showing the way of escape: the plan of salvation, following the Way, the Truth, the Life — The Lord Jesus Christ — and the eventual removal of the curse, and no more sorrow, pain, tears or death, enjoying eternity in heaven with our Savior!

3. Continuous Appeal

Here is a book, old with antiquity, but it absolutely refuses to grow old! Every time I read the Bible, it makes me feel a little younger. Sometimes I think I just may have found the fountain of youth! Here is a book of many yesterdays, that's as new as today, and it holds all our tomorrows. When I read it, I sometimes feel that I don't have to worry so much about tomorrow, because I know Who holds tomorrow, and He is already there! He tells me in His Word: "Let not your heart be troubled…" (John 14:1); "Fear not…" (Isaiah 41:10); and "Be careful [anxious] for nothing…" (Philippians 4:6).

This Book of God delights ALL! It's the all-time Best Seller of All Ages — for All Ages! For young and old and in-between! For Children – Zacheus climbed a sycamore tree, and David and Goliath; for Youth – Joseph, and his principles teaching how to resist evil; the three Hebrew children and Daniel, show how to stand tall for God, love Him and serve Him. For Adults – to model after Jesus, Paul and Peter, finding answers to vexing problems; and for Seniors – to enjoy all that the children, youth and adults do, plus, they overdose on the COMFORT portion! And the 23rd Psalm!

It's Inexhaustible – The Bible never runs dry, it's never stale but always fresh. You read it, reread it, and it still seems new. The more you read it, the more you want to read it! Those who know it best, love it most. One can't say this about any other book!

A Never-Failing Source of Inspiration – for Art, Music and Literature. Poets, authors, composers, and artists draw heavily from its pages. Not to mention it's a source for education and even higher education. The Bible was actually used as a textbook in our nation's earliest schools. Our first colleges were started by and supported by churches. Churches and compassionate Bible-believing people started our first hospitals, e.g. Methodist, St. Vincents, and St. Francis!

It Laughs at and Defies the Laws of Literature: 1) Death must come to all books. 2) Ancient books are not acceptable to modern times, except as museum pieces. The Bible is the most ancient of books, yet it still intrigues, challenges, and inspires keen modern minds. 3) Jewish books do not interest Gentile readers. The Bible was written by Jewish men, yet its greatest appeal is to the Gentile world! We don't actually think of the Bible as Jewish. It seems like our very own because we know and love the Author so much. 4) The Law of the Best Seller: they sell great for a year or so, some a few years, maybe even ten, then most fade. The Bible, the Book of God, has been the Best Seller for centuries!

As a matter of fact, it's well-known that the Bible is the ALL-TIME BEST SELLER and has been translated into over two thousand languages! A little-known fact: **the Bible is the Best-Selling Book of the year...EVERY YEAR!** "The Bible is the world's Best-Selling book of all time and the best-selling book of the year, every year! Fifty Bibles are sold every minute. It's never shown on the best seller lists because it dwarfs the sales of all other books."[3] **A book can rise no higher than its source.** The Bible's **Source** is the **Most High God!**

A Best Kept Secret!

At the end of the last century, *Life* magazine published ***The Life***

Millennium: the 100 Most Important Events and People of the Past 1,000 Years, **covering the years 1001 to 2000**. The results were nothing short of miraculous — proof positive that the Bible is God's Word, God's Book!

You are thinking, *surely not, you're not telling us that in the past millennium, the last 1,000 years, something about the Bible was rated in the "100 Most Important Events,"* as rated by a liberal news media source that cancels conservatives, Christians, and anything to do with the Bible. (Oh, you say, it's probably about prayer and Bible reading being banned from public schools by the Supreme Court in 1962 and 1963.)

Let's just cut to the chase and **go to the "Top Ten Events!"** No way, you say! Wait. Are you sitting down? To save time, let's go to the **"Top Three Events!"** Are you ready? **Start the Countdown: #3. Martin Luther**, in 1517, nails his "95 Theses" to the door of a Catholic church in Wittenberg, Germany, beginning the Reformation! **#2. Christopher Columbus** discovers a new world in 1492!

Life's **#1 Most Important Event of the Past 1,000 Years!**

It's time for a drumroll and a trumpet fanfare as you **fasten your seat belts and raise your Bibles High!** (Remember, a book can rise no higher than its source.) To prove that the source of the Bible is the Most-High God, and that **God Gave the Word**:

#1. "Gutenberg Prints the Bible!" in 1455!

This is God! God did this! He inspired the Bible to be written, miraculously preserved it, providentially guided Gutenberg to print it, and Life editors to rate it the # 1 Most Important Event of the Past 1,000 years! God Gave the Word, the Bible, and it became available to the common man: to every man, woman, and child! God just made the world bow down and do obeisance to the fact that this is God's Book. *Life* credited this event for ushering in the Renaissance, the Protestant Reformation, and the Industrial Revolution. And "He unleashed an information epidemic that rages to this day."

It gets better: Gutenberg was absent from the top one-hundred men of the past Millennium. So, his name was not a factor in the #1 ranking of this event. We're left with the "Printing of the Bible" as the #1 Most Important Event of the past Millennium! No other book would have ranked # 1. *Life* just acknowledged that the Bible is God's Book! **This miraculous event is proof positive that the Bible is God's Word!**

The Supreme Court "cancelled" Bible reading in public schools in 1963, but God had the last laugh. And He will continue to have it when, on Judgement Day, He will, without doubt, "cancel" the "cancel culture court justices" that did it.

Why does the Bible have all this continuous appeal and inspiration? Because its Author is God, not man. The Bible is not our book about God — it's God's Book about us! The words are living and powerful! Hebrews 4:12 says, "For the Word of God is quick [alive] and powerful, sharper than any two-edged sword..." Once again—a book can rise no higher than its source, and the Bible's source is the **Most High God!**

4. Unparalleled Teachings

You would expect a Book from God to be different. For crystal-clear proof of the Bible's claim to unique, unparalleled teaching, just simply READ it! Words seem to leap from the page: as you meditate, it actually SPEAKS to your heavy heart, your broken heart, and it comforts you. You find answers to life's many problems, and as you continue reading and searching the Scriptures, you will find eternal life!

Who has not been wonderfully moved and blessed by everyone's favorite Bible passage, the great **23rd Psalm**? And, oh, the lofty teachings of the Sermon on the Mount, and the Beatitudes. In high school, the beautiful chapter on Charity/Love, 1 Corinthians 13, was part of my senior literature studies! (How times have changed!) "Though I speak with the tongues of men and of angels, and have not charity, I am become as sounding brass or a tinkling cymbal" (1 Corinthians 13:1).

This Holy Book of God's phenomenal teachings deals with vital subjects that we need to know about, and no other religion's books even dare touch on them (because they don't have the answers): subjects like the origin of the universe, and planet earth, of life, of man, and of evil. And the origin of satan, death, and of life after death and eternity. This book alone gives authoritative answers to these vital subjects.

What supreme, unparalleled LITERATURE content! Do you like biographies? Read the best four biography books ever written: Matthew, Mark, Luke, and John! Do you thirst for action and drama? Don't miss the action in the ACTS (of the Apostles)! Are you a military history buff? March right to Joshua and Judges. Do you have a yearning for emotional, poetic writings? Fly to the Book of Psalms. Need wisdom? Apply at Proverbs and Ecclesiastes. Looking for romance with surprise endings? Esther and Ruth are must reads. Are you curious about all those origins mentioned above? For starters, try Genesis, the book of beginnings. So you think you have it rough? Don't miss Job, and the four gospels on the life of Jesus.

How do you get saved? Read Acts, and then *act* accordingly. How do you stay saved? Read the Epistles (letters to the churches), Romans through Jude. For answers to the biggest, most important questions of all—PROPHECIES of what the future holds, and who wins in the end—camp in the book of Revelation! The Bible covers it all: the holiness of God, the sinfulness of sin, man's fall, the Gospel of the good news of the plan of salvation through Jesus' Name, Born Again, Acts 2:38 Salvation, and our eternal destinies!

God's Book easily sees all: past, present, and future. No other book comes close to comparing! Its teachings are unmatched by any others. They are clearly unparalleled and unprecedented!

5. Scientific Accuracy

True, the Bible is not a science book, but when it touches on science it is accurate. The first three words in the Bible have now been widely accepted by many scientists as being scientific: "In the beginning…" (Genesis 1:1). Scientists believe that the universe is winding down, stars are dying, and eventually the universe will die completely, called a uniform heat death. Then it had to have had a beginning (the Big Bang theory), because if it had been in existence for all eternity past, as some scientists postulated in the "steady state" theory, it would have already died. Many scientists, not just Bible-believing scientists, now believe that the first *four* words, "In the beginning God..." are scientific, because this fine-tuned universe full of complex intelligence (e.g. DNA) could not create itself from nothing by chance, random mistakes. Evolution, in summary, says, "First there was nothing, it exploded, and now we have everything." Is that scientific? If there was nothing, then there was nothing to explode! An "explosion" created all this complex design and beauty? Explosions create destruction, not order, design, and beauty. Astronomer Fred Hoyle thought the likelihood that this complex creation was produced by chance, was equal to the likelihood that "a tornado sweeping through a junkyard might assemble a Boeing 747 from the materials therein."[4]

The Law of First Causes, aka the Law of Cause and Effect, states that no effect can be greater than its cause. We have planet earth, full of life, love, beauty, consciousness, reason, intelligence, and the ability to appreciate all of it. The First Cause of such a marvelous creation must be greater than the creation, it must be a transcendent, Supreme Being that is Himself alive, loving, conscious, intelligent, full of reason, all to a greater degree than what He created, because science says the cause must be greater than the effect! This marvelous creation could not have come about by chance!

We go back to the first chapter of Genesis for true science: God ordained that each basic "kind" of life was to reproduce "after his kind." (Fifteen times!) This has been proven by the laws of genetics, and the laws of heredity, and proven true down through time. The Genesis "kinds" were a broader category than "species," probably closer to the "family" category in the classification system. This allowed for some genetic variation, but there are fixed limits beyond which they can't cross, whether cross breeding dogs, or roses, or Gregor Mendel's peas. We can get different varieties of roses but never an orchid or tulip from a rose; we can get different varieties of dogs but never a cat from a dog. The same is true in the fossil record. There is no record of changing from one kind of life to another. There are no transitional forms showing changing from invertebrates to vertebrates (creatures with backbones), or from fish to amphibians, or from reptiles to birds! So, the fossil record supports the Genesis account of creation and shouts, "No!" to "molecules to man" evolution. Genesis was right: "After his kind!"

The Bible is Scientifically Accurate

Psalm 8:8 was the basis for the discovery of ocean currents! This phrase "… whatsoever passeth through the paths of the sea," leaped out at naval oceanographer Matthew Maury, and he set out to map out the ocean currents, with the help of charts and records on file and conversations with shipmasters. (See figures 1 and 2). Maury was called, "Pathfinder of the Seas," and "Father of Modern Oceanography!" How did Psalmist David know about the "paths of the sea," ocean currents, almost three thousand years before they were discovered?

Matthew Maury — Pathfinder of the Seas

Figure 1

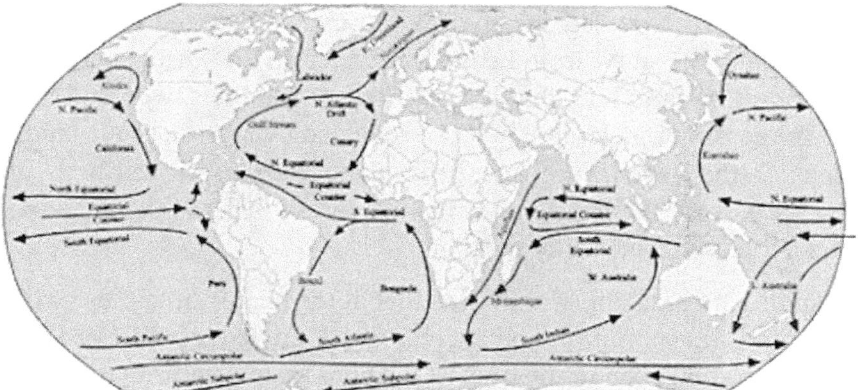

Figure 2 — Ocean Currents

The most famous ocean current, the *Gulf Stream*, is a vast moving mass of water, transporting an enormous amount of heat from the Caribbean across the ocean to Europe.

Isaiah 40:21-22 states that the earth is round! "Have ye not understood from the foundations of the earth? It is he that sitteth upon the circle of the earth...." How did Isaiah know this over two thousand years before Copernicus and Galileo?

"For the life of the flesh is in the blood..." (Leviticus 17: 11) proved that life was in the blood, and blood circulation was a key factor thirty-five hundred years before medical science began to catch up (William Harvey, 1600's). Doctors used to drain the blood from the sick to get rid of the "poison" causing the sickness; they even attached leeches to suck the blood!

It was amazing that God gave Moses the principles of sanitation, hygiene, and dietetics, long before they were proven scientifically correct. Moses had to have it to march three million people, living in close quarters, for forty years across the desert wilderness! It is also amazing that the Bible was written in a non-scientific environment, yet none of the false theories crept in! The Bible agrees with the facts of science but not with some of the theories and hypotheses, which change often.

Isaiah 55:10 revealed the hydrologic cycle: "As the rain cometh down, and the snow from heaven ... watereth the earth, and maketh it bring forth and bud, that it may give seed to the sower, and bread to the eater." And Jeremiah 10:13 revealed evaporation: "... and he causeth the vapours to ascend from the ends of the earth ... and bringeth forth the wind out of his treasures." All of this has proven the Bible is scientifically accurate!

Daniel 12:4 amazingly predicted that at the end of time there would be rapid transportation and increase of knowledge! "O Daniel, ... seal the book, even to the time of the end: many shall run to and fro, and knowledge shall be increased." For almost fifty-nine hundred years the fastest a man could move was on horseback! Then steam engines, trains, cars, airplanes, jets, rocket ships, man on the moon, and now shooting for Mars, all in one hundred fifty to two hundred years! "**Many shall run to and fro.**" Daniel may have seen interstate traffic through and around Los Angeles, Chicago, Atlanta, and New York City.

"**Increase of knowledge**!" With the invention of computers, the internet, and smart phones, we have tons of info right at our fingertips. It used to take one hundred years for all knowledge to double. Scientists have now estimated the "Knowledge Doubling Curve." In 1900, knowledge was doubling every one hundred years; by 1945, every twenty-five years. And by 1982, due to the advent of personal computers, it was doubling **every twelve months!** That was forty years ago. What do you think the knowledge doubling rate is today?

Fasten your seat belts! IBM predicted a few years ago that the doubling of knowledge would transition from linear growth to an *exponential growth*, due to leading-edge computer technology combined with artificial intelligence (AI), and the Internet with fifty billion interconnected devices, and Big Data (modern data analytics with collaborating teams sharing knowledge), so that by 2020, knowledge would double **every twelve *hours*!** This **knowledge explosion** is being called a **TSUNAMI!** (See figure 3) This is mind-boggling! Daniel wrote, "**At the time of the end…knowledge shall be increased**!" Could it be any clearer?

This proves three things! **1)** The **Bible** is **scientifically accurate**, and **2)** we are living "**at the time of the end!**" It is also, **3)** a phenomenal example of **fulfilled prophecy**! (How could Daniel have known this almost twenty-six hundred years before it happened?)!

The Coming Knowledge Tsunami[5]

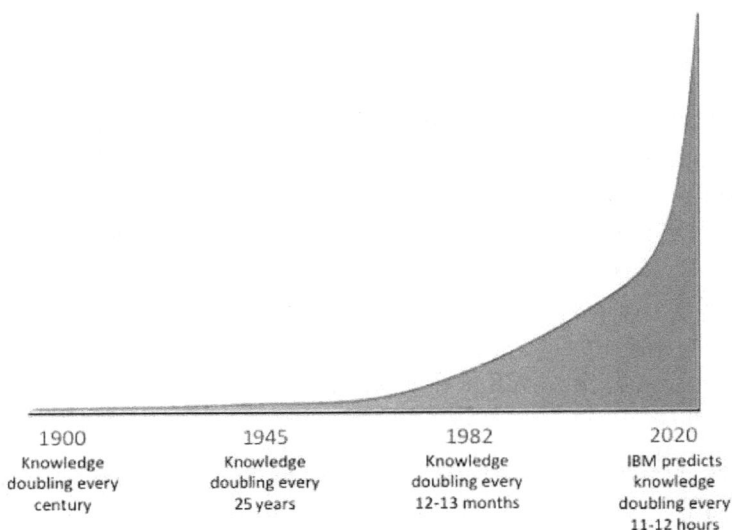

1900	1945	1982	2020
Knowledge doubling every century	Knowledge doubling every 25 years	Knowledge doubling every 12-13 months	IBM predicts knowledge doubling every 11-12 hours

The knowledge explosion

Figure 3: **Buckminster Fuller's Knowledge Doubling Curve, with post-1982 addition by IBM**

At the top right of the above graph, we shall confidently write, "**The time of the end**" from Daniel's prophecy of **Daniel 12:4!**

"And that, knowing the time, that now it is high time to awake out of sleep: for now is our salvation nearer than when we believed" (Romans 13:11). With the knowledge of the fulfillment of Daniel 12:4 resonating in our souls, we must agree with the apostle Paul, we know the time and it's high time to awake out of sleep for our salvation is very near! It is imperative that we be **Woke on the WORD!**

Why a Seven-Day Week?

Here is another astounding proof of the accuracy of Genesis and the Bible. Today man counts time based on astronomy: one day is the length of time for the earth to rotate on its axis, twenty-four hours; one year is the length of time for the earth to revolve around the sun: 365¼ days; and one month approximates the length of time for the moon to revolve around the earth. But the seven-day week has no basis in astronomy whatsoever! So why does the whole world keep time in seven-day weeks, and when and where did it start?! Why not a week of ten days? The obvious answer: it has carried over from Genesis, chapter one!

The seven-day week is a remnant of Genesis, Chapter One, and the whole world is bowing down and acquiescing to this great truth of God's Book. It has continued ever since the beginning of time. Noah kept track on the Ark, and, after the confusion of tongues at the Tower of Babel and the scattering of the nations, all nations and cultures continued counting time in seven-day weeks! To God be the glory!

Science vs. The Bible

One of the most common fallacies today is the belief that science and the Bible conflict. This view is tragically wrong. Thousands of scientists of the past and present have been and still are Bible-believing Christians. In fact, many philosophers of science and discerning historians have recognized that the founding fathers of modern science were Bible believers who maintained they "were thinking God's thoughts after Him." The very existence of modern science had its origins in a culture committed to a biblical basis at a time in history marked by a great return to biblical faith. *True* science is never at enmity with God.

Founders of Modern Science – Great Scientists Who Believed the Bible

Leonardo da Vinci (1452 - 1519) Considered by many to be the real founder of modern science, a great engineer, architect, and incomparable painter, his scientific notebooks are filled with studies and analyses in dynamics, anatomy, physics, optics, biology, hydraulics, even aeronautics, all far in advance of his time. The Renaissance man was **rated by *Life* magazine 5th in the 100 most important people of the last millennium!** His masterpieces of art, *Mona Lisa* and *The Last Supper*, a painting that has blessed and stirred the souls of millions over the centuries, bear witness to his faith in the Bible.

Johann Kepler (1571 – 1630) Considered to be the founder of physical astronomy, he discovered the laws of planetary motion and conclusively demonstrated the sun, not the earth, was the center of the solar system. He contributed to the eventual development of calculus. He was the first scientist to state that in his astronomical research, he was merely "thinking God's thoughts after him," a motto adopted by many believing scientists since his time. Kepler wrote in one of his books, "Since we astronomers are priests of the highest God in regard to the book of nature, it befits us to be thoughtful, not of the glory of our minds, but rather, above all else, of the glory of God."

Isaac Newton (1642 – 1727) Most scholars have judged Sir Isaac Newton to have been the greatest scientist who ever lived! He discovered the Law of Gravity, formulated the three laws of motion, the basis of modern mechanics and dynamics, developed calculus into a comprehensive branch of mathematics, now a basic tool in every science. He anticipated the great law of energy conservation and constructed the first reflecting telescope. *Life* **magazine rated him 6th in the 100 most important people of the last millennium,** saying, "A passionately religious man…[he] wanted to know how God's universe worked."[6] He wrote strong papers refuting atheism and defending Creation and the Bible. He believed that the worldwide flood of the Bible accounted for most of the geological phenomena, and he believed in the literal six-day creation. He said, "We account the Scriptures of God to be the most sublime philosophy. I find more sure marks of authority in the Bible than in any profane history whatsoever."[7]

Louis Pasteur (1822 – 1895) One of the greatest names in the history of science and medicine, most scientists today would say he was the greatest biologist of all time. He established the germ theory of disease, developed vaccines, and founded the modern science of immunology, saving countless lives. He developed pasteurization, sterilization, and conclusively demolished the pet concept of evolutionists: spontaneous generation (that life could come from non-life.) He was opposed by almost the entire biological establishment because of his opposition to Darwinism. A strongly religious man, *Life* **magazine rated him 8ᵗʰ in the 100 most important people of the last millennium!**[8]

Samuel F. B. Morse (1791 – 1872) Famous for his invention of the telegraph, he gave us a new way to communicate. *Life* **magazine rated him 39ᵗʰ in the 100 most important people of the last millennium!**[9] His first message over the wire, in 1844, using his Morse code, was a Scripture out of the Bible, Numbers 23:23, "What hath God wrought!" He was also an outstanding artist. He wrote: "The nearer I approach to the end of my pilgrimage, the clearer is the evidence of the divine origin of the Bible, the grandeur and sublimity of God's remedy for fallen man are more appreciated, and the future is illumined with hope and joy."

Joseph Lister (1827 – 1912) His great contribution was the development of antiseptic surgery through use of chemical disinfectants. Probably second only to Pasteur in terms of saving human lives. *Life* **magazine rated him 43ʳᵈ in the 100 most important people of the last millenium!**[10] A humble and gracious man of Quaker background, he wrote, "I am a believer in the fundamental doctrines of Christianity."

Michael Faraday (1791 – 1867) Universally acknowledged as one of the greatest physicists of all time, he laid the groundwork for the electrical age, developing the new sciences of electricity and magnetism. *Life* **magazine rated him 70ᵗʰ in the 100 most important people of the last millennium**! He discovered electromagnetic induction, invented the generator, designed an electric motor, a prototype for those that drive everything from subways to vacuum cleaners. A member of a small fundamentalist church whose teaching emphasized God's creation as purposeful and harmonious, and designed for man's well-being, he fully believed in the official doctrine of the church which said, "The Bible, and it alone, with nothing added to it nor taken away from it by man, is the sole and sufficient guide for each individual, at all times and in all circumstances..."[11]

Charles Babbage (1792 – 1871) A fascinating scientist, in many respects far ahead of his time. A mathematician, he developed the first actuarial tables, invented the first speedometer, the first skeleton keys, and the first ophthalmoscope. Most importantly, he developed the first true computer, including the use of punched-card directions and information storage and retrieval systems. As a Christian he wrote the ninth and last of the Bridgewater Treatises, a remarkable apologetic including a mathematical analysis of the Biblical miracles.

Wernher von Braun (1912 – 1977) He was one of the world's top space scientists. With a Ph.D. from the University of Berlin, he was a leading German rocket engineer, developing the famed V-2 rocket during WWII. He migrated to the U.S. in 1945, became a U.S. citizen in 1955, was the chief architect in the development of the Saturn V rocket, became director of NASA, and helped put man on the moon in Apollo 11! He was a Lutheran, active in church and Christian life. In a foreword to an anthology on creation and design in nature, he gave this testimony, "Manned space flight is an amazing achievement, but it has opened for mankind thus far only a tiny door for viewing the awesome reaches of space. An outlook through this peephole at the vast mysteries of the universe should only confirm our belief in the certainty of its Creator..."[12]

6. Archaeology

In Luke 19:39-40, when the Pharisees asked Jesus to rebuke His disciples for their loud praises, "He answered and said unto them, I tell you that, if these should hold their peace, the stones would immediately cry out." Well, some must not have been praising Him loud enough, because the rocks and stones have been crying out in praise to God for many decades now, through archaeology, proving the Bible is true and the biblical record is confirmed beyond a doubt. It has now been documented that there was a high degree of civilization, culture, and writing well before 2000 B.C., before the time of Moses, which was one of the early criticisms by archaeologists. Skeptics also claimed that there was no Hittite civilization until archaeologists digging in modern Turkey discovered the records and documented it. They also found the Walls of Jericho, and they fell outward just as described in the Bible, and one section stood—where Rahab and her family were safe!

Skeptics claimed Sargon and Belshazzar never existed. They thought Belshazzar was a mythical personage in their criticism of the book of Daniel. But archaeological discoveries proved they both existed, and Belshazzar did rule over Babylon, just as the book of Daniel said, as co-regent, while his father, Nabonidus, historians proved, was away in Arabia on an archaeological reconstruction project.

John McRae, professor of archaeology, and author of *Archaeology and the New Testament,* said there's no question that archaeological findings have enhanced the New Testament's credibility. Josh McDowell, in his book, *More Evidence that Demands a Verdict,* lists twenty-two pages of archaeological discoveries, and he writes, "In summary, archaeological discoveries show at point after point that the biblical record is confirmed and commended as trustworthy. This confirmation is not confined to a few general instances."[13]

William F. Albright, outstanding twentieth century archaeologist, declared, "There can be no doubt that archaeology has confirmed the substantial historicity of the Old Testament."[14] Dr. Norman Geisler, author of more than sixty books on Christian apologetics, said, "There have been thousands of archaeological finds in the Middle East that support the picture presented in the biblical record." Discoveries supporting King David, Abraham, Isaac, and Jacob have increasingly corroborated them. Evidence for Sodom and Gomorrah uncovered a great conflagration. Every reference to an Assyrian king has been proven correct. An excavation during the 1960s confirmed that, yes, they could enter Jerusalem by way of a conduit, a tunnel, during David's reign. They have uncovered evidence that the world did have a single language at one time. The site of Solomon's Temple has now been excavated.

Noted Roman historian Colin J. Hemer shows how archaeology has confirmed hundreds and hundreds of details from the early church, thus confirming the accuracy of the New Testament record. Luke was a physician and an impeccable historian who wrote the Book of Acts. Even small details of his writing have been confirmed: like how deep the water was a certain distance from the shore, and what kind of disease a certain island had. Luke has been proven right in hundreds of details and never proven wrong in writing the whole history of Jesus and the early church!

Great Oxford University classical historian, A. N. Sherwin-White said, "For Acts, the confirmation of history is overwhelming" and that "any attempt to reject its basic historicity must now appear absurd."[15]

Rocks and stones also cry out in another very conspicuous way in proof of (fasten your seat belt) **Noah's Flood!** This earth is covered with thousands of layers of sedimentary strata, water-laid rock layers, all over the world. (Yes, you've seen these exposed rock layers while driving the interstates when they blasted through a hill instead of going over it to lay the road). And they contain vast fossil graveyards with billions of fossils that were trapped in the sediments of a one-time, great, world-wide cataclysm: giving conclusive proof to many Creationist Scientists of **Noah's flood** that destroyed the earth and all that had the breath of life on it, except for the occupants of the Ark. (See AnswersinGenesis.org, the Creation Museum and the Ark Encounter in the Cincinnati, OH area).

So, in the field of archaeology, thousands of silent witnesses have been resurrected to TESTIFY to the TRUTH of the Bible record. The *rocks and stones do cry out*, through archaeological discoveries, confirming the Bible is the true Word of God!

7. Fulfilled Prophecy

The Bible is the only book in the world that has precise, specific predictions (prophecies) made hundreds of years in advance, that were literally fulfilled to the letter. Thus, the Bible has credentials absent from all other religious books and texts, such as the Quran of Islam. That makes fulfilled prophecy one of the greatest proofs that the Bible is the inspired Word of God! The Bible boldly and confidently gives thousands of prophetic predictions. And not just in vague generalities but in detailed specifics.

In Daniel 2, God revealed to King Nebuchadnezzar in a dream (known as Nebuchadnezzar's Image), the four Gentile World Empires. They started with himself, as the head of gold: the Babylonian empire. And then history filled in the names of the empires as they occurred: the Medo-Persian led by Cyrus the Great, the Greek empire led by Alexander the Great, and finally the vast Roman empire.

We have already looked at Daniel 12:4, Daniel's end-time prophecy regarding many running to and fro and the increase of knowledge; this is currently being fulfilled, showing clearly that we are living in "the time of the end."

The dispersion and scattering of the Jews was prophesied by many prophets. The Jews completely lost their homeland for almost two thousand years. It is humanly impossible that a nation could retain its identity that long without a homeland. And even more so that they could return and establish their ancient nation once again: "And it shall come to pass in that day, that the Lord shall set his hand again the second time to recover the remnant of his people…and shall assemble the outcasts of Israel and gather together the dispersed of Judah from the four corners of the earth" (Isaiah 11:11-12). This was fulfilled May 14, 1948, shortly after WWII, when Israel became a nation.

Probably the most convincing proofs of all are the hundreds of Old Testament prophesies of Christ, giving a detailed portrait of His birth, life, death, burial, and resurrection.

The birth of the New Testament church was prophesied in Joel 2:28, "And it shall come to pass afterward that I will pour out my spirit upon all flesh…." This amazing prophecy was fulfilled dramatically on the Day of Pentecost in the New Testament, and Peter quoted from it in Acts 2:16-17: "But this is that which was spoken by the prophet Joel; And it shall come to pass in the last days, saith God, I will pour out of my Spirit upon all flesh…." Peter went on to preach: "Then Peter said unto them, Repent, and be baptized every one of you in the name of Jesus Christ for the remission of sins, and ye shall receive the gift of the Holy Ghost" (Acts 2:38). Then in the next verse, Peter prophesied, "For the promise is unto you, and to your children, and to all that are afar off, *even* as many as the Lord our

God shall call" (Acts 2:39). We know this is true prophecy, for it has been fulfilled in many of our lives! Of course, there are numerous other prophecies; this is just a small sampling.

Peter Stoner and other mathematicians have calculated the probability that one man could fulfill the many detailed prophecies (over three hundred) of Christ's first coming. They came up with an astronomical number of one chance in ten to the 157th power for just forty-eight of the prophecies. That's ten followed by one hundred fifty-seven zeroes! That's too vast to even comprehend. It would take the divine hand of an Omnipotent God to orchestrate it. And He did! This is absolute, indisputable evidence that the Bible is God's Word!

In Isaiah 41:23, the prophet challenged the heathen gods: "Show the things that are to come hereafter, that we may know that ye are gods." Well, God has accepted this challenge and shown through prophecy many things to come hereafter, so *we would know without a doubt that He is God!* The odds of so many prophecies being fulfilled by any one person are far, far beyond the realm of possibility and the law of probability! **Fulfilled prophecy** is thus one of the most substantiated proofs that the Bible is the inspired (God-breathed), infallible, inerrant Word of God!

All the prophecies about the Lord's first coming to earth were fulfilled perfectly! Question? There are many prophecies about the Lord's second Coming! Do you think they will be fulfilled? Absolutely!

> For the Lord himself shall descend from heaven with a shout, with the voice of the archangel, and with the trump of God: and the dead in Christ shall rise first: Then we which are alive *and* remain shall be caught up together with them in the clouds, to meet the Lord in the air: and so shall we ever be with the Lord.
>
> 1 Thessalonians 4:16-17

So Christ was once offered to bear the sins of many; and unto them that look for him shall he appear the second time without sin unto salvation.

Hebrews 9:28

Behold, I shew you a mystery; We shall not all sleep, but we shall all be changed, In a moment, in the twinkling of an eye, at the last trump: for the trumpet shall sound, and the dead shall be raised incorruptible, and we shall be changed. For this corruptible must put on incorruption, and this mortal *must* put on immortality. So when this corruptible shall have put on incorruption, and this mortal shall have put on immortality, then shall be brought to pass the saying that is written, Death is swallowed up in victory. O death, where *is* thy sting? O grave, where *is* thy victory?

1 Corinthians 15:51-55

We know with absolute certainty that all these prophecies of Christ's second coming will be fulfilled precisely because all the prophecies of His first coming were fulfilled to the letter!

8. The Witness of Jesus and the Bible's Internal Witness

A. Jesus Verified the Old Testament

Some don't believe the early chapters of Genesis are literal. They want to believe that Adam and Eve were myths, an allegory, in an attempt to harmonize the Bible with evolution and thus escape facing God for judgement. One of the most convincing proofs for the historical accuracy of Genesis is that the Lord Jesus Christ himself regarded it as such, as did also the Apostle Paul, writer of half the New Testament!

> The Pharisees also came unto him, tempting him, and saying unto him, Is it lawful for a man to put away his wife for every cause? And he answered and said unto them, Have ye not read, that he which made *them* at the beginning made them male and female, And said, For this cause shall a man leave father and mother, and shall cleave to his wife: and they twain shall be one flesh?
>
> Matthew 19:3-5

Here, Jesus quoted from Genesis 1:27 and 2:24, thus confirming the historicity of Genesis! He put His seal of approval on Genesis and Moses' writings! He also referred to Abel, Lot, Noah, and Jonah as historically true people, not myths! Paul also quoted Genesis 2:24 in Ephesians 5:31.

> Think not that I am come to destroy the law, or the prophets: I am not come to destroy, but to fulfil. For verily I say unto you, Till heaven and earth pass, one jot or one tittle shall in no wise pass from the law, till all be fulfilled.
>
> Matthew 5:17-18

In this passage of Scripture "jot" is "iota," the smallest letter in the Greek alphabet; "tittle" is a small curl on letters to distinguish them from other letters.

> Then he said unto them, O fools, and slow of heart to believe all that the prophets have spoken: Ought not Christ to have suffered these things, and to enter into his glory? And beginning at Moses and all the prophets, he expounded unto them in all the scriptures the things concerning himself.
>
> Luke 24:25-27

> And he said unto them, These *are* the words which I spake unto you, while I was yet with you, that all things must be fulfilled, which were written in the law of Moses, and *in* the prophets, and *in* the psalms, concerning me. Then opened he their understanding, that they might understand the scriptures.
>
> Luke 24:44-45

Here, Jesus was speaking to the Apostles just before He ascended. The Jews divided the Old Testament into three divisions: the law, the prophets, and the Psalms. In these Scriptures Christ verified the authenticity of the entire Old Testament!

> If he called them gods, unto whom the word of God came, and the *scripture cannot be broken*....
>
> John 10:35 (italics added for emphasis)

> For had ye believed Moses, ye would have believed me: for he wrote of me. But if ye believe not his writings, how shall ye believe my words?
>
> John 5:46-47

Here, Jesus equated Moses' writing to His words. This is why the devil hates and attacks the early chapters of Genesis. He is still sowing doubt and lies to undermine the Gospel of Christ.

The Apostle Paul got on board, confirming the veracity of Adam as a real historical person in Romans 5:12-14, "Wherefore, as by one man sin entered into the world, and death by sin; and so death passed upon all men, for that all have sinned...Nevertheless death reigned from Adam to Moses..." So, we clearly see that Adam was a real historical figure, as real as Moses! Paul settled the debate once and for all with 1 Corinthians 15:21-22, "For since by man came death, by man came also the resurrection of the dead...For as in Adam all die, even so in Christ shall all be made alive." Now we clearly see how that deleting Adam undermines the Gospel of Christ. Do away with Adam and his fall into sin, causing death, and we no longer need a Savior to deliver us and resurrect us from the dead. Adam and Christ are inextricably linked. In fact, Jesus was called, "the last Adam" (1 Corinthians 15:45). The first Adam was a "figure [a type] of him that was to come," the last Adam (Romans 5:14). It's no wonder our adversary wants to do away with any belief in the first Adam. He could thereby "cancel" belief in the last Adam, Jesus Christ.

B. Jesus Verified the New Testament

"But the Comforter, *which is* the Holy Ghost, whom the Father will send in my name, he shall teach you all things, and bring all things to your remembrance, whatsoever I have said unto you" John 14:26). Jesus pre-authenticated the New Testament before it was written: the Holy Ghost will teach you all things and help you remember what I said. They would not be recording their remembrances and recollections, but the Holy Ghost's!

"Howbeit when he, the Spirit of truth, is come, he will guide you into all truth: and he will shew you things to come" (John 16:13). Jesus clearly taught the Holy Ghost would guide them into all truth and show them things to come. God was going to show the Apostles further truth through the Holy Ghost. We can confidently accept all apostolic writing, teachings, and doctrines as divinely inspired! And, the same God who inspired the writing, also controlled the selection and collection: which writings were chosen for the New Testament Canon, comprising the Bible. (See also #9 Preservation).

"But he answered and said, It is written, Man shall not live by bread alone, but by every *word* that proceedeth out of the mouth of God" (Matthew 4:4, emphasis added). By every "word," not just every thought. The New Testament gives us Jesus' Words!

C. The Bible's Internal Witness

"All scripture *is* given by inspiration of God, and *is* profitable for doctrine, for reproof, for correction, for instruction in righteousness" (2 Timothy 3:16). The phrase "given by inspiration of God" is one word in the Greek, *theopneustos*, meaning "God-breathed." Not just the thoughts are God-breathed, but the words written down, the actual writings! **God Gave the Word!**

> Knowing this first, that no prophecy of the scripture is of any private interpretation. For the prophecy came not in old time by the will of man: but holy men of God spake *as they were* moved by the Holy Ghost.
>
> 2 Peter 1:20-21

"Prophecy" refers not only to predictions of the future but also to any divinely inspired utterance—therefore to all Holy Scriptures. The Spirit of God "moved" the hearts, minds, and tongues of Holy men of God and the Scriptures were formed by the mind and will of God, not by the mind or will of men. God used different styles and traits of the writers, but the truths were carefully clothed in words from God because they were inseparable. But the will of man had nothing to do with it. **God Gave the Word!**

> Heaven and earth shall pass away: but my words shall not pass away.
>
> Luke 21:33

> For ever, O LORD, thy word is settled in heaven.
>
> Psalm 119:89

Inspired "Words"

"Now to Abraham and his seed were the promises made. He saith not, And to seeds, as of many; but as of one, And to thy seed, which is Christ" (Galatians 3:16). Paul makes an exceedingly strong argument to affirm the verbal inspiration of the Old Testament Scriptures, basing it not just on one word, but on one *letter*, "s," and whether it said, "seed" singular, or "seeds" plural! Again, "one jot or one tittle shall in no wise pass from the law till all be fulfilled.

"Which things also we speak, not in the *words* which man's wisdom teacheth, but which the Holy Ghost teacheth; comparing spiritual things with spiritual" (1 Corinthians 2:13, emphasis added). The NIV, emphasis added, renders, "but in *words* taught by the Spirit, explaining spiritual realities with *Spirit-taught words*." **The Holy Ghost teaches with "words!"** David said, in 2 Samuel 23:2 (emphasis added), "The Spirit of the LORD spake by me, and his *word was* in my tongue." The prophet Jerermiah said, "Then the LORD put forth his hand, and touched my mouth. And the LORD said unto me, Behold, I have put my *words* in thy mouth" (Jeremiah 1:9, emphasis added). Bible writers unanimously declare, the *words* came from God—they were just agents, the messengers! **God gave the Word!**

9. Miraculous Preservation

No other book has such a history of persecution and opposition—yet it remains the all-time best seller, for God has miraculously preserved His Book. The giving of the Word was a miracle and so also is the preservation of it! Not only have evil men sought to destroy it, but it has also been bitterly hated by Satan and the powers of darkness. Yet in the face of unparalleled and unprecedented persecution, the Bible stands stronger today than ever before. Isaiah prophesied in Isaiah 40:8, "The grass withereth, the flower fadeth: but the word of our God shall stand for ever." And again, Jesus proclaimed, "Heaven and earth shall pass away: but my words shall not pass away" (Luke 21:33).

Consider the hurdles: The Babylonian captivity in 606 BC: Judah was carried captive into Babylon for seventy years. Those precious Bible manuscripts were in danger of being lost! Some unknown, unsung hero(es) preserved them! A **Miracle!**

While the church was still young, there was a severe Roman persecution of the Christians under Nero in AD 64. Then the temple and Jerusalem were destroyed by Roman general Titus Vespasian in AD 70. All this happened while the New Testament was in the process of being written, and they were trying to preserve the Old Testament! Then in AD 135 Jerusalem was completely destroyed, and the Jews were completely dispersed, scattered among all nations, known as the Diaspora, fulfilling Bible prophecy. Through all this God's faithful, protecting hand shielded and guarded the Holy Scriptures! A multitude of **Miracles!**

The Roman emperor, Diocletian, in AD 303, used the political and military might of the Roman empire to try to stamp out the Bible and Christianity. He issued a medal proclaiming Christianity was destroyed, with the inscription, "The Christian religion is destroyed and the worship of the Roman gods is restored." But Jesus said His words would not pass away, and "the gates of hell shall not prevail against [the church]" (Matthew 16:18). A **Miracle!**

Next, the world descended into the "Dark Ages," from about AD 500 to AD 1000. Bibles were in essence imprisoned in the musty darkness of medieval churches and monasteries, but the Reformation heroes arose and began to liberate the Word of God. **More Miracles!** Gutenberg perfected the printing press and began printing the first Bibles in 1455, and thus, put the Bible in the hands of common, ordinary men, thanks to Bible translators like John Wycliffe, William Tyndale and Miles Coverdale who translated the Bible into English, in the 1300s, 1400s, and 1500s! **More Miracles!**

Three hundred years later the attacks continued, this time from within. Skeptics, even liberal ministers, began trying to explain away the miracles through natural means. "Scholars" began using new techniques of destructive criticism called "higher criticism," trying to undermine confidence in the inspiration and authenticity of the Bible. Since this was an attack from Satan, it should have been called "lower" criticism. But modern heroes soon sprang to the rescue to defend the Bible and give answers to the criticisms. They were called Apologists and wrote "Apologetics," which meant they gave answers and gave a defense for the Bible. Also, archaeologists came to the rescue, and scientists that were Creationists showed the flaws and weaknesses in Darwinian evolution, showing that it was, to the honest and unbiased, impossible. Time and time again, the Bible has been vindicated! It was truly a **Miraculous Preservation!**

A history of notable miracles has kept this Holy Book preserved. God has determined that all the world shall most assuredly hear the gospel of Christ! He is "… not willing that any should perish, but that all should come to repentance" (2 Peter 3:9).

Voltaire

We can't leave out Voltaire, the famous French philosopher, who railed against Christianity and the Bible with poisonous venom, calling it the "infamous superstition." He predicted in 1776, "One hundred years from my day, there will not be a Bible on earth except one that is looked upon by an antiquarian curiosity seeker. We're living in the twilight of the Bible and Christianity. The Bible will be known only as a relic of antiquity."[16] (I had heard this story before and decided to research it online.) There is a lot of information, both pros and cons. But I found an extensive article about this story on "CrossExamined.org." by Dr. Daniel Merrit, in an essay about "Voltaire's Prediction." Dr. Merrit fully documented the quote, giving much credible information from letters with details, names, dates, etc. There can be no doubting it. Now, for the rest of the story:

Voltaire died two years later in 1778, and in 1836, fifty-eight years after his death, his former home in Geneva, Switzerland, was serving as a storehouse for Bibles and gospel tracts. The Evangelical Society did not own the house, but Col. Henri Tronchin, President of the Society, lived there, and he used some of the rooms to store the Bibles which Voltaire so vehemently opposed. Furthermore, on the very printing press which Voltaire employed to print his irreverent works, at Ferney, France, editions of the Bible were printed. It gets better. The Bibles were printed on a special paper especially made for a superior edition of Voltaire's works. But his project failed, so the paper was bought and devoted to a higher purpose—the printing

GOD GAVE THE WORD

of the Word of God. He was proven to be a false prophet and once again, God had the last laugh! The Bible is the world's All-Time Best Seller, and remains the Best-Selling Book of the Year, every single year!

In 1998, *Life* Magazine published, *The Life Millennium, The 100 Most Important Events and People of the Past 1,000 Years.* **Life selected as the #1 event of the past 1,000 years: #1, Gutenberg Prints the Bible!**

Would someone please tell me how the most hated and persecuted book in the world became the #1 best seller of all time (and every single year), and the printing of it by Gutenberg in 1455 was chosen the singular most important event of the last millennium!? There can be only one explanation: **God Gave the Word! The Bible is God's Book!**

"The words of the LORD are pure words: as silver tried in a furnace of earth, purified seven times. *Thou shalt keep them, O LORD, thou shalt preserve them* from this generation for ever" (Psalm 12:6-7, emphasis added).

10. Transforming Power

This Book absolutely can and will change and transform people's lives. It is no exaggeration to say, multiplied millions of miracles have taken place in the lives of men, women, and children simply by reading, believing, trusting, and obeying the Words of this Book! The weak receive strength, cowards become heroes, lovers of evil become lovers of good and of God, the downcast are uplifted, slaves to sin and bondage are set free, chains broken; and grief-stricken mourners and broken-hearted are greatly comforted, the lost are saved, and the dead are brought back to life! Those that have made a complete mess of their lives are BORN AGAIN of the water and Spirit (John 3:5 and Acts 2:38-39) and filled with rejoicing at getting a brand-new start on life!

2 Corinthians 5:17 says, "Therefore if any man *be* in Christ, *he is* a new creature: old things are passed away; behold, all things are become

new." John 1:12 states, "But as many as received him, to them gave he power to become the sons of God, *even* to them that believe on his name...." There is POWER in this! TRANSFORMING POWER! Hebrews 4:12 (emphasis added) says "For the word of God *is* quick, [alive] and *powerful*, and sharper than any two-edged sword, piercing even to the dividing asunder of soul and spirit, and of the joints and marrow." Romans 10:17 declares, "So then faith *cometh* by hearing, and hearing by the word of God." Hearing the Words of this BOOK produces FAITH, which TRANSFORMS LIVES! "Wherewithal shall a young man cleanse his way? by taking heed *thereto* according to thy word" (Psalm 119:9). And it still works for all ages, not just for the young! Furthermore, He "is able to do exceeding abundantly above all that we ask or think, according to the *power* that worketh in us" (Ephesians 3:20, emphasis added)!

It *changes* people! It causes missionaries to leave homes and comfortable lifestyles, to forsake family and friends, luxury, security, and go to the unknown, and suffer loneliness, untold hardships, some even buried their children. There is something about this Book, this Word of God, that gets in people and changes them—transforms them into new creatures in Christ!

We have all felt this transforming power and "have tasted of the heavenly gift, and were made partakers of the Holy Ghost, and have tasted the good Word of God, and the powers of the world to come..." (Hebrews 6:4-5)! We have an experience with God and have actually "tasted the good Word of God!" So, people with an experience are never at the mercy of a skeptic with an argument. As Evangelist Lee Stoneking says, "We've got it, and we know we've got it!"

Everywhere this Bible has gone and been respected and believed, schools, colleges and hospitals have sprung up! At the beginning of our nation the Bible was the main textbook in most of our first elementary schools!

Colleges: Most of the first colleges in colonial days were started by and supported by churches and were Bible-centered: Harvard, Yale, and Dartmouth by the Puritans; Princeton by the Presbyterians; Rutgers by the Dutch Reformed; College of William and Mary by

GOD GAVE THE WORD

the Church of England. And there are still over six hundred Christian colleges today, many of them are major institutions: Notre Dame, Georgetown, Brigham Young, Liberty, Columbia, Duke, Baylor, Southern Methodist, TCU, Oral Roberts, Indiana Wesleyan, and Urshan College & Graduate School, and our very own IBC (Indiana Bible College) in Indianapolis, which started in Seymour, IN, at the church where I attend.

Hospitals: Bible-believing Christians have been leaders in medicine, caregiving, and building hospitals: such as Methodist (IU Health) in Indianapolis, and St. Vincents, and St. Francis. The modern hospital system owes its existence in large part to compassionate believers in the Bible, caring people of Faith! After all, it all started in AD 30 with Jesus healing people, and the origins of hospitals and care giving have continued through the compassionate Judeo-Christian culture.

Some may complain that we put entirely too much emphasis on the Bible, and that we place it too high on a pedestal, practically worshipping it, almost making an idol out of it. Is that possible? Psalm 138:2 proclaims, "For thou hast magnified thy word above all thy name." We proudly and rightly hold the matchless Name of Jesus in high esteem! We even call ourselves, "The people of the Name!" But God just said that He MAGNIFIES HIS WORD **above** His Name! We cannot love His Word too much! Without His Word we would not even know His Name! His Word has, in fact, REVEALED HIS NAME!

In SUMMARY: We found regarding the Bible: 1) **Highly Reasonable and a Necessity** that God would give us a Book to guide us, and we looked at several proofs; 2) **Amazing Composition;** 3) **Continuous Appeal**; 4) **Unparalleled Teachings**; 5) **Scientific Accuracy**; 6) **Archaeology**; 7) **Fulfilled Prophecy**; 8) **The Witness of Jesus and the Bible**; 9) **Miraculous Preservation**; 10) **Transforming Power!**

Any one of these ten reasons could easily stand alone as adequate, with more than sufficient evidence to prove the authenticity of the Bible as God's Word. But these ten reasons, taken altogether, prove conclusively, beyond the shadow of a doubt, that **this Holy Bible is the Book of God! It is His Book!** The evidence is overwhelming and incontrovertible! **God Gave the Word!** And isn't it wonderful that we may *have it, hold it in our hands, clasp it to our hearts, read it, study, it, memorize it, sing it, quote it, pray it, LOVE it, weep over it, and rejoice over it!* The Bible truly is **God's Love Letter** to us, our **Guidebook, Manufacturer's Handbook, Compass, Roadmap, GPS!** "**A Lamp** unto our feet, and a **Light** unto our path" **(Psalm 119:105)! God Gave the Word! We would be lost without it! But with it, we are SAVED!**

"I have a wonderful treasure, it's given to me without measure;

And so we'll travel together, my Bible and I!"

WOKE ON THE WORD

The amazing book of Daniel is the second most rejected book by Bible critics and skeptics (Genesis being the first), because it is loaded with remarkably fulfilled prophecies. For example, Nebuchadnezzar's Image, revealing the four Gentile world empires, and Daniel's Seventy Weeks, showing the Messiah cut off after sixty-nine weeks (four hundred eighty-three years), and the remaining yet-to-be-fulfilled, one week (seven year) tribulation period. But Daniel 12:4 is a rarely mentioned, yet very important, Old Testament prophecy that many believe is currently being fulfilled, showing clearly that the coming of the Lord is imminent.

"The Time of the End"

Daniel 12:4 records, "But thou, O Daniel, shut up the words, and seal the book, even to the time of the end: many shall run to and fro, and knowledge shall be increased." At the time of the end, many, probably all over the world, will be running to and fro and racing back and forth. It's fascinating to realize that for about fifty-eight hundred years (using Ussher's chronology), the fastest a man could move (race) was on a swift horse (thirty mph). Then, in the early 1800's the steam engine was invented, and by 1830 the train. By 1886 we had the car, and by 1903 the airplane (the Wright brothers at Kitty Hawk, NC, a 12 second flight). Then, the race began in earnest. In the next sixty-six years, man went from faster planes to jets, to breaking the sound barrier (seven hundred sixty-seven mph) in 1947, to rocket ships: the Saturn V, speeding fifteen thousand five hundred mph to get into orbit, and twenty-five thousand mph in reaching the moon! In 1969, Apollo 11 put a man on the moon! From "twelve seconds" to the moon in just sixty-six years! Phenomenal!

A graph illustrating the fulfillment of this prophecy would show a long, flat line representing fifty-eight hundred years at a maximum speed of thirty mph on a swift horse. Then, in a mere sixty-six years, from 1903 to 1969, the line would rapidly rise and soar exponentially off the chart! That rise occurred in the last 1% of our timeline. And we are still soaring, now pointing for the planet Mars. Thank you, Daniel, for telling us what time it is. We will write, *"The time of the end!"* at the top of our graph!

"Knowledge Shall Be Increased."

Scientists have studied the "Knowledge Doubling Curve" to determine how long it takes for the total amount of human knowledge to double. They estimated that by 1900, knowledge was doubling every one hundred years. By 1945, it was doubling every twenty-five years. By 1982, due to the advent of personal computers in the late 70s and early 80s, knowledge was doubling every twelve to thirteen *months! Time* magazine called 1982, "The Year of the Computer." That was over forty years ago. What has happened since then? A lot: the Internet, the World Wide Web, and smartphones and other devices connected to the Internet!

So, how fast is knowledge doubling now? In 2013, IBM reported that due to leading-edge computer technology, combined with Artificial Intelligence allowing collective problem solving on a larger scale, and due to the Internet with fifty *billion* interconnected devices, and with Big Data (modern data analytics with collaborating teams sharing knowledge), all of this would result in the creation of vast amounts of knowledge. Thus, IBM predicted that by 2020, knowledge doubling would **explode** to, not every twelve weeks, not every twelve days, but, incredibly, every **twelve *hours*!** The graph was titled: **The Coming Knowledge Tsunami!**[17] (See figure 3, page 28) Could it be any clearer? "To the time of the end…knowledge shall be increased." We KNOW exactly what time it is…

It's Time to Wake Up

Romans 13:11 says, "And that, knowing the time, that now it is high time to awake out of sleep: for now, is our salvation nearer than when we believed." We are "now" most assuredly at "the time of the end," fulfilling Daniel 12:4. Yes, we're "awake" in a certain sense, reading our Bibles, praying, fasting, faithful to church, worshiping and feasting on the preaching of the Word, witnessing, winning, discipling, etc.. But do these alone constitute being completely spiritually awake? When Paul said, "Now it is high time to awake out of sleep..." he surely meant for us to be fully awakened and aware of the times we are living in and to have a deep understanding of the Word of God in relation to them. It is imperative that we be Woke on the Word!

Asleep at the Wheel

At the birth of Christ, a group of very religious people, especially the scribes and doctors of the law, had the Word. They had Micah 5:2 telling **where** the Messiah would be born: in Bethlehem, and they told the Wise Men. They had Daniel 9:24-26 telling approximately **when** the Messiah would be born: in Daniel's "70 Weeks" prophecy Messiah would be cut off after sixty-nine weeks (69 x 7 = 483 years). The "70 Weeks" timeclock started ticking at "the going forth of the commandment to restore and to build Jerusalem" (Daniel 9:25) which occurred about four hundred forty-five years earlier. So, yes, it's time for the Messiah to be born! They had Isaiah 7:14, telling **how** the Messiah would be born: of "a virgin!" They had Isaiah 9:6 telling **who** the Messiah would be: "the mighty God"! They had Isaiah 53 and 61 telling **why** He would come: to suffer for them, and to set them free! So, they should have followed the Wise Men to Bethlehem and made diligent inquiry. They were the chosen people of God, and they had the Word, but they were asleep and missed it. How indescribably sad that God's chosen people missed the first coming of Jesus. God forbid that the chosen generation of His Bride be slumbering and miss His Second Coming.

How to Awaken

How can we become fully awake to God's Word? **Read it, read it, read it!** Don't rush. Instead, slow down and meditate. The Lord commanded Joshua, "Thou shalt meditate therein day and night... observe to do according...then thou shalt make thy way prosperous, and then thou shalt have good success" (Joshua 1:8). Feast on the **preaching** of the Word! Be a hearer and a doer (James 1:22). **Memorize** it! Hide it in our hearts so we won't sin against God. (Psalm 119:11). **Pray the Word!** And **Worship** in spirit and truth (John 4:24), aware of the Word embedded in our lively songs and exuberant worship.

Sleepwalking

It was the third day, and the two were journeying back to Emmaus. Jesus Himself drew near, but they didn't recognize Him. When He asked why they were so sad, they told him briefly about Jesus' crucifixion, how they had trusted He was the Messiah, and now His body was missing. "Then he said unto them, O fools, and slow of heart to believe all that the prophets have spoken: Ought not Christ to have suffered these things, and to enter into his glory? And beginning at Moses and all the prophets, he expounded unto them in all the scriptures the things concerning himself" (Luke 24:25-27). They constrained Him to stay and have dinner with them. Verse 30 records, "And it came to pass, as he sat at meat with them, he took bread, and blessed it, and brake, and gave to them."

Awakened with a Heartburn

At that precise moment, a most wonderful thing happened---an awesome awakening! "And their eyes were opened, and they knew him; and he vanished out of their sight" (Verse 31). They literally awakened to the Living Word. Jesus was the Word [God] made flesh. (John 1:1, 14). "And they said one to another, Did not our **heart burn** within us, while he talked with us by the way, and while he opened to us the scriptures?" (Verse 32). When He opened to them the Scriptures they awakened to the Written Word also, and their hearts were burning with a wonderful, stirring, joyous, gotta-tell-somebody spirit! They had to share this with the rest of the disciples!

"Get your sandals back on!" "But it's eight miles back to Jerusalem." "Well, there will be no sleep for us tonight. We are **wide awake!**" "And they rose up the same hour and returned to Jerusalem..."

(Verse 33), with burning hearts that were vibrantly awake to both the Living Word and the Written Word. Thus, being awake on the Word and burning hearts appear to be synonymous, occurring simultaneously as the Lord opens to us His Word and we awaken with hearts ablaze.

The Ultimate "Woke on the Word!"

"For the Lord himself shall descend from heaven with a *shout*, with the *voice* of the archangel and with the trump of God: and the dead in Christ shall rise first:" (The ultimate "Woke on the Word" moment!) "Then we which are alive and remain shall be caught up together with them in the clouds, to meet the Lord in the air: And so shall we ever be with the Lord. Wherefore comfort one another with these words." (1 Thessalonians 4:16-18, emphasis added).

Knowing the time, that now it is high time to be Woke on the Word, may our hearts burn within us, as never before, as He opens to us the Scriptures, in Jesus' Name!

Ron Schoolcraft

God's Mighty Weapons

Okay, the bad news first: we are at war. The good news? We have weapons, and they are mighty through God. And we win! The apostle Paul admonished us, "We do not war after the flesh: (For the *weapons* of our warfare are not carnal, but *mighty through God* to the pulling down of strong holds)" (2 Corinthians 10:3-4, emphasis added) Weapons and weaponry are also called "arms." 2 Corinthians 10:4 could very well be called "the 2nd Amendment for Christians!" It gives us the absolute right to keep and bear arms, to use God's mighty weapons in spiritual warfare. Paul stressed that these were "weapons of *our* warfare." They are ours to keep, bear, and use, and this right shall not be infringed by Satan and his minions.

Our Adversaries

Paul revealed our formidable foes in Ephesians 6:12, "For we wrestle not against flesh and blood, but against principalities, against powers, against the rulers of the darkness of this world, against spiritual wickedness in high places." ("...in the heavenly realms." NIV). This is spiritual warfare against evil spiritual forces: Satan and his fallen angels. Before revealing some of our weapons, Paul expressly commanded us to "suit up" in verse 11, "Put on the whole armour of God, that ye may be able to stand against the wiles of the devil." Protective armor such as breastplates, shields, and helmets are indispensable in this war to quench Satan's fiery darts (flaming arrows).

"Take the Sword"

The armor of God continues in Ephesians 6:17, "And take ... the sword of the Spirit, which is the word of God." Finally, an offensive weapon and it's not just a sword, but the "sword of the Spirit," clearly identified here as the "word of God." The "word" here is the Greek *rhema,* meaning the individual saying or text. We need to unsheathe and brandish this sword of the Spirit like Jesus did when tempted by Satan in the wilderness.

Weaponizing the Word

Jesus told Satan, "It is written," three times in Matthew 4:4-10. Each time He quoted the Word of God, the individual saying. He was pointing the Word of God in Satan's face like a sword. Jesus changed the Word into a sword: the sword of the Spirit! He weaponized the Word! When Satan taunted Him to turn the stones into bread, Matthew 4:4 records, "But he answered and said, It is written, Man shall not live by bread alone, but by every word [again, Greek *rhema*] that proceedeth out of the mouth of God." This is the Word of God we hold in our hands and hide in our hearts. Jesus finally dispatched the devil by once again weaponizing the Word of God into the sword of the Spirit. "Then saith Jesus unto him, Get thee hence, Satan: for it is written, Thou shalt worship the Lord thy God, and him only shalt thou serve. Then the devil leaveth him ..." (Matthew 4:10-11). Some may say that Satan fled because that was Jesus speaking, but we can't do it. The Word of God is the sword of the Spirit regardless of who speaks it. Jesus has *already* spoken it or inspired (God-breathed) it into existence. That's why it is "the Word of God," for us to weaponize. And now that Matthew 4:10-11 "is written," we shall not fail to add it to our arsenal of "weapons ... mighty through God." Thus, "It is written, Get thee hence, Satan ...."

The "Sharper" Sword

Hebrews 4:12 echoes, "For the word of God is quick [alive], and powerful, and sharper than any twoedged sword, piercing even to the dividing asunder of soul and spirit, and of the joints and marrow...." The word of God is alive, powerful, sharper, and piercing. It sounds like a sword! But it's much more than a sword. It's "sharper" than a natural, double-edged sword or a surgeon's scalpel. It is in truth, "the sword of the Spirit," one of God's mighty weapons.

A Second Weapon in the Armor?

Yes, the armor of God reveals another of God's mighty weapons in Ephesians 6:18: "Praying always with all prayer and supplication in the Spirit, and watching thereunto with all perseverance and supplication for all saints." Prayer is a vital part of the armor of God and well-deserving of its position at the pinnacle of the arsenal of God's mighty weapons. Perhaps one reason for "praying always" is because the Lord desires to *answer* always. We should also, "Pray without ceasing" (1 Thessalonians 5:17), so He can answer without ceasing.

Prayer "War-riors"

Epaphras is one of the Bible's unsung heroes. "Epaphras, ... always labouring fervently for you in prayers..." (Colossians 4:12). "Labouring fervently" is one word in the Greek, *agonizomai*, from which we get our English word "agonize." (NIV: "... always wrestling in prayer ..."). This same word is translated "fight" in 2 Timothy 4:7, "I have fought a good fight." Prayer should never be considered a "behind-the-scenes" effort. It is a front-line, in-the-trenches, hand-to-hand combat, spiritual fight against a hindering adversary. It is laboring fervently, agonizing, wrestling, fighting, as well as travailing and interceding. Not by coincidence are they called "war-riors." Prayer warriors are indispensable in our warfare. James 5:16 confirms, "The effectual fervent prayer of a righteous man availeth much." Prayer is one of God's mighty weapons. Prayer warriors are God's mighty weapons!

Join the Resistance

James gave us a general purpose, all-occasion, "go to" Scripture for resisting the devil: "Submit yourselves therefore to God. Resist the devil, and he will flee from you" (James 4:7). Just resist — push back! This is what Jesus did in the wilderness temptation. He could have easily zapped Satan, reducing him to a pile of ashes. But He used the sword of the Spirit, the word of God, to resist him, thus giving us an example. He did not ask us to pummel the devil but to resist him. Let us use this word, James 4:7, as the sword of the Spirit, and the devil "will flee from you." Note: James said to, first, "Submit yourselves *therefore* to God" (emphasis added). "Therefore" refers to the preceding verse, James 4:6: "God resisteth the proud, but giveth grace unto the humble." We must, therefore, be humble, not proud and arrogant.

The apostle Peter also enjoined us to "Join the Resistance" in 1 Peter 5:8-9, "Be sober, be vigilant, because your adversary the devil, as a roaring lion, walketh about, seeking whom he may devour: Whom resist stedfast in the faith." Again, just resist, push back, and now we may use this word as the sword of the Spirit. Peter also stressed humility, two verses earlier: "Humble yourselves therefore under the mighty hand of God, that he may exalt you in due time" (1 Peter 5:6). Humility is key, as we note in the attitude of the archangel Michael when contending with the devil (Jude 9). If we will humble ourselves under the mighty hand of God, He will arm us with the mighty weapons of God.

Weapons Galore

The Word of God is replete with exceeding great and precious Scriptures to weaponize as "weapons of our warfare." Here are a few: Matthew 16:18, "… upon this rock I will build my church; and the gates of hell shall not prevail against it." Isaiah 54:17, "No weapon that is formed against thee shall prosper." Jeremiah 51:20, "Thou art my battle axe and weapons of war: with thee will I destroy kingdoms." 2 Corinthians 10:5, "Casting down imaginations, and every high thing that exalteth itself against the knowledge of God, and bringing into captivity every thought to the obedience of Christ." Luke 10:19 says, "Behold, I give unto you power to tread on serpents and scorpions, and over all the power of the enemy."

And Still More:

John 8:44, "... the devil ... is a liar, and the father of it." 1 John 4:4, "... greater is he that is in you, than he that is in the world." Romans 8:31, "If God be for us, who can be against us?" Matthew 6:13, "... lead us not into temptation but deliver us from evil." Isaiah 59:19, "When the enemy shall come in like a flood, the Spirit of the LORD shall lift up a standard against him." Mark 16:17, "And these signs shall follow them that believe; In my name shall they cast out devils." Colossians 2:14-15, "... nailing it to his cross; And having spoiled principalities and powers, he made a shew of them openly, triumphing over them in it." Hebrews 2:14, "... that through death he might destroy him that had the power of death, that is, the devil." And Isaiah 58:6, "Is not this the fast that I have chosen? to loose the bands of wickedness, to undo the heavy burdens, and to let the oppressed go free, and that ye break every yoke?" Thus, fasting is also one of God's mighty weapons! This catalog of weapons barely scratches the surface. Please add your favorites.

Armageddon: The Ultimate Sword in Action

Revelation 19:21 says, "The remnant were slain with the sword of him that sat upon the horse, which sword proceeded out of his mouth." It is noteworthy that in Matthew 4:4, man is to live "by every word that proceedeth out of the mouth of God," which word, in Ephesians 6:17, is "the sword of the Spirit," "which sword" in Revelation 19:21, "proceeded out of his mouth." We just came full circle with a tri-fold confirmation that causes us to triumph! We win! May God help us tap into the power of "weapons ... mighty through God."

The Prophet of Pentecost: "Prepare War"

Joel prophesied Pentecost in chapter 2 of his book (Joel 2:28). He prophesied war in chapter 3: "Prepare war, wake up the mighty men...let the weak say, I am strong" (Joel 3:9-10). We have the mighty weapons of God (2 Corinthians 10:4), and "the mighty God"

(Isaiah 9:6). All we need is a few "mighty men!" We do have them, and even now they are waking up and preparing for war. May God call mighty men, women, soldiers, and warriors who are consumed with zeal, to do battle for God, to take the battle to the enemy, and to storm the gates of hell, pulling down strongholds, reaping the harvest and rescuing the perishing. We shall use God's mighty weapons, and we shall be victorious. "Through God we shall do valiantly: for he it is that shall tread down our enemies" (Psalm 60:12).

Ron Schoolcraft

ON THE BATTLEFIELD

Gen. George S. Patton's Warfare Tactics

The apostle Paul often used the analogy of military warfare to teach us principles of Christian, spiritual warfare. He told Timothy to "... endure hardship as a good *soldier* of Jesus Christ. No one engaged in *warfare* entangles himself with the affairs of this life, that he may please him who *enlisted* him as a *soldier*" (2 Timothy 2:3-4, NKJV, emphasis added). He exhorted us to "... put on the whole *armour* of God, that ye may be able to stand against the wiles of the devil" (Ephesians 6:11, emphasis added). He then detailed each piece of military armor and weaponry (breastplate, shield, helmet, and sword) and gave their spiritual parallels (Ephesians 6:13-17).

While recently reading *War As I Knew It*, the battlefield memoirs of that swashbuckling World War II General, George S. Patton, Jr., I was struck by the spiritual parallels in his unique battlefield tactics. Maybe we can profit spiritually as General Patton's 3rd Army and the Allied Forces did militarily.

Though somewhat controversial for his flamboyance, outspokenness, profanity, and uncompromising standards, Patton was fundamentally a profoundly religious man who read the Bible daily. Using an aggressive combat strategy, he slammed the tanks and men of the Third Army across Europe at a breakneck pace. Patton's armored force moved farther and faster than any other in World War II, ensuring his place in history as one of the greatest battlefield commanders. He felt we could end the war by Christmas, 1944, (saving five months and many lives) if he was given gas for his tanks and "turned loose" to attack and destroy the retreating enemy army.

Marching Fire

General Patton gave clear instructions for advancing into enemy territory: marching fire—the proper way to advance was to use marching fire and keep moving. "One round should be fired every two or three paces. The whistle of the bullets, the scream of the ricochet, and the branches and twigs knocked from the trees would have a terrifying effect on the enemy. The soldiers must keep walking forward. Shooting adds to their self-confidence, because they're firing, not sitting like a duck in a bathtub being shot at."[18]

Of course, the Christian's offensive weapon is "the sword of the Spirit, which is the word of God" (Ephesians 6:17). As we storm the gates of hell to do battle with the forces of evil to rescue souls, we, too, need to use "marching fire," shouting the Word of God in prayer as we march forward. "…behold, I will make my words in thy mouth fire" (Jeremiah 5:14). "Let the high praises of God be in their mouth and a twoedged sword in their hand" (Psalm 149:6). "And he hath made my mouth like a sharp sword…" (Isaiah 49:2).

Fire Back

General Patton knew war was often a matter of life and death. He preached that to halt under fire was folly. To halt under fire and not fire back was suicide. His directive was to move forward out of the fire. And always remember that it was much better to waste ammunition than lives. He knew that it took at least eighteen years to produce a soldier, but only a few months to produce ammunition. When under a spiritual assault from the enemy, we must continue to "fire back" with the Word of God as Jesus did to Satan when He said, "It is written..." in the temptation in the wilderness (Matthew 4:1-11). Thank God we need not fear running out of scriptural ammunition, and it is never wasted, for it will not return void (Isaiah 55:11).

Best Defense? Go Forward Fast!

General Patton was not a proponent of digging foxholes and trenches. He preached: wars are not won by defensive tactics. Digging is primarily defensive. The psychological effect on the soldier is bad, because if he thinks he must dig in, he must think the enemy is dangerous, which he usually is not. Patton probably preferred singing "Onward Christian Soldiers" rather than "Hold the Fort."

Patton thought the expression "hit the dirt" did much to increase casualties. Only on rare occasions would he permit dropping. He specified that even then he must not hit the dirt and stay supine. He must shoot fast at the enemy, because "it is as true now as when Farragut stated it in the Civil War that the 'best armor (and the best defense) is a rapid and well-directed fire.' When soldiers are caught in a barrage, from mortars, rockets, or artillery, the surest way to get out of it is to go forward fast,"[19] because the enemy artillery very seldom shortens its range.

No wonder the German army feared Patton. His message was "Forward, March." The answer to almost all dilemmas was: "Go forward fast!" Christians have a similar command and commission: "Go ye into all the world, and preach the gospel to every creature" (Mark 16:15), "Go ye therefore, and teach all nations" (Matthew 28:19), and "I charge you therefore before God ... Preach the word" (2 Timothy 4:1-2). As we march forward firing salvoes of the salvation message of Acts 2:38, "No weapon that is formed against thee shall prosper" (Isaiah 54:17). We should not tarry, but go forward fast: "Say not ye, There are yet four months, and then cometh harvest? Behold I say unto you, Lift up your eyes, and look on the fields; for they are white already to harvest" (John 4:35).

Don't Delay

The battlefield genius of this formidable general is revealed in this instruction to officers in his command: "Don't delay — the best is the enemy of the good. By this I mean that a good plan violently executed *now* is better than a perfect plan next week. War is a very simple thing, and the determining characteristics are self-confidence, speed, and audacity. None of these things can ever be perfect, but they can be good."[20]

The "speed" is up to us. If we wait until everything is perfect: we are debt free, understand all mysteries, wear a halo, etc., we may never reap the harvest. May we catch the vision of the psalmist, "He sends out his command to the earth; His word runs very swiftly" (Psalm 147:15, NKJV); and of Joel, "Prepare war, wake up the mighty men, let all the men of war draw near. Put ye in the sickle, for the harvest is ripe" (Joel 3:9,13).

Enlist Now

May God inspire and enable us for immediate and massive action utilizing the firepower of God's Word in preaching, teaching, evangelizing, winning, and discipling: "For the word of God is quick, and powerful, and sharper than any twoedged sword, piercing even to the dividing asunder of soul and spirit, and of the joints and marrow, and is a discerner of the thoughts and intents of the heart" (Hebrews 4:12).

General Patton thought that all other forms of human endeavor shrank to insignificance when compared to war. He wrote to his wife, near the end of the war, that peace was going to be very difficult for him. Could we be as zealous in our Christian warfare? May God grant us thousands of "Pentecostal Pattons" to be valiant warriors for God.

"Through God we shall do valiantly: for he it is that shall tread down our enemies" (Psalm 60:12).

The Beatitudes in the Old Testament

Psalm 1:1-3 "**Blessed is the man** that walketh not in the counsel of the ungodly, nor standeth in the way of sinners, nor sitteth in the seat of the scornful. But his delight is in the law of the LORD; and in his law doth he meditate day and night. And he shall be like a tree planted by the rivers of water, that bringeth forth his fruit in his season; his leaf also shall not wither; and whatsoever he doeth shall prosper."

Psalm 2:12 "... **Blessed are all they** that put their trust in him."

Psalm 32:2 "**Blessed is the man** unto whom the LORD imputeth not iniquity, and in whose spirit there is no guile."

Psalm 34:8 "O taste and see that the LORD is good: **blessed is the man** that trusteth in him."

Psalm 40:4 "**Blessed is that man** that maketh the LORD his trust, and respecteth not the proud, nor such as turn aside to lies."

Psalm 41:1-2 "**Blessed is he** that considereth the poor: the LORD will deliver him in time of trouble." The LORD will preserve him, and keep him alive; and he shall be blessed upon the earth: "

Psalm 65:4 "**Blessed is the man** whom thou choosest, and causest to approach unto thee, that he may dwell in thy courts: we shall be satisfied with the goodness of thy house, even of thy holy temple."

Psalm 84:5 "**Blessed is the man** whose strength is in thee; in whose heart are the ways of them."

Psalm 84:12 "O LORD of hosts, **blessed is the man** that trusteth in thee."

Psalm 89:15 "**Blessed is the people** that know the joyful sound: they shall walk, O LORD, in the light of thy countenance."

Psalm 94:12 "**Blessed is the man** whom thou chastenest, O LORD, and teachest him out of thy law;"

Psalm 106:3 "**Blessed are they** that keep judgment, and he that doeth righteousness at all times."

Psalm 112:1 "**Blessed is the man** that feareth the LORD that delighteth greatly in his commandments."

Psalm 119:1 "**Blessed are the undefiled** in the way, who walk in the law of the LORD."

Psalm 119:2 "**Blessed are they** that keep his testimonies, and that seek him with the whole heart."

Psalm 128:1 "**Blessed is every one** that feareth the LORD; that walketh in his ways."

Proverbs 8:32 "Therefore hearken unto me, O ye children: for **blessed are they** that keep my ways."

Proverbs 8:34 "**Blessed is the man** that heareth me, watching daily at my gates, waiting at the posts of my doors."

Isaiah 30:18 "And therefore will the LORD wait, that he may be gracious unto you, and therefore will he be exalted, that he may have mercy upon you ... **blessed are all they** that wait for him."

Isaiah 32:20 "**Blessed are ye** that sow beside all waters, that send forth thither the feet of the ox ..."

Jeremiah 17:7 "**Blessed is the man** that trusteth in the LORD, and whose hope the LORD is."

Ron Schoolcraft

A Time to be Selfish?

Praise God for His awesome saving and keeping power! This essay shall in no way minimize or detract from God's sovereign power. Yet, the Scriptures are replete with instructions reminding us that, after God saves us, there are things we can and should do in paying attention to our "selves," even examining ourselves to see whether we are in the faith (2 Corinthians 13:5). The following ten tips are a sample:

1. Take heed to thyself - "Take heed unto **thyself**, and unto the doctrine" (1 Timothy 4:16). This great proof-text for the importance of doctrine shows that taking heed to "thyself" is as necessary as taking heed to the doctrine. It takes both. This verse concludes, "continue in them: for in doing this thou shalt both save **thyself**, and them that hear thee." Clearly, taking heed to ourselves is absolutely essential.

2. Save yourselves - "Save **yourselves** from this untoward generation" (Acts 2:40). Of course, we know that God saves us, but He doesn't force us or drag us to Him kicking and screaming against our will. He knocks, but we must answer. As Max Lucado has said, "If there are a thousand steps between us and Him, He will take all but one. But He will leave that final one for us. The choice is ours."[21]

3. Delight Thyself - "Delight **thyself** also in the LORD; and he shall give thee the desires of thine heart" (Psalm 37:4). We not only love the Lord and believe, trust and obey Him, but we are blessed to delight ourselves in Him! "Then shalt thou delight **thyself** in the LORD; and I will cause thee to ride upon the high places of the earth" (Isaiah 58:14). He will grant our desires!

4. Cleanse ourselves - "Having therefore these promises, dearly beloved, let us cleanse **ourselves** from all filthiness of the flesh and spirit, perfecting holiness in the fear of God" (2 Corinthians 7:1). We would do well to work diligently, in the fear of God, at perfecting holiness by separating and cleansing ourselves from any pollutants that would contaminate or defile our flesh and spirit. What are "these promises" that we will receive if we cleanse ourselves? "I will receive you, and will be a Father unto you, and ye shall be my sons and daughters, saith the Lord Almighty" (2 Corinthians 6:17-18). Can you think of any greater promises?

5. Submit yourselves - "Submit **yourselves** therefore to God. Resist the devil, and he will flee from you" (James 4:7). The all-important first step in resisting the devil, our cunning adversary, is to submit ourselves to God. Further, "Yea, all of you be subject one to another, and be clothed with humility: for God resisteth the proud, and giveth grace to the humble" (1 Peter 5:5).

6. Humble yourselves - "Humble **yourselves** in the sight of the Lord, and he shall lift you up" (James 4:10). And again, "Humble **yourselves** therefore under the mighty hand of God, that he may exalt you in due time" (1 Peter 5:6). The proximity of these passages on humility to the scriptures on resisting the devil suggests that humility may indeed be a vital component of devil-resisting (see James 4:6-10 and 1 Peter 5:5-9.) "If my people, which are called by my name, shall humble themselves, and pray…" (2 Chronicles 7:14).

7. Arm yourselves - "Forasmuch then as Christ hath suffered for us in the flesh, arm **yourselves** likewise with the same mind: for he that hath suffered in the flesh hath ceased from sin" (1 Peter 4:1). We should expect some suffering and arm ourselves with the mind of Christ to endure it. Longsuffering is, after all, a part of the fruit of the Spirit (Galatians 5:22). "For unto you it is given in the behalf of

Christ … to suffer for his sake" (Philippians 1:29). Let us also arm ourselves with: "the sword of the Spirit, which is the word of God," as well as with the whole armor of God (Ephesians 6:13-17).

8. Assemble ourselves - "Not forsaking the assembling of ourselves together, as the manner of some is..." (Hebrews 10:25). We must stand fast against the increasingly popular trend in these "busy" times to assemble ourselves less, lest we be disassembled (dispersed and scattered). This verse concludes, "but exhorting one another: and so much the more, as ye see the day approaching." David said, "One thing have I desired of the Lord, that will I seek after; that I may dwell in the house of the Lord all the days of my life, to behold the beauty of the Lord, and to inquire in his temple" (Psalm 27:4).

9. Keep yourselves - "Keep yourselves in the love of God" (Jude 21). The preceding verse gave explicit instructions on how to keep ourselves in His love: "But ye, beloved, building up yourselves on your most holy faith, praying in the Holy Ghost" (Jude 20). If we will keep ourselves in His love by building up ourselves in faith, by praying in the Holy Ghost, then we can safely leave the rest to: "him that is able to keep you from falling, and to present you faultless before the presence of his glory with exceeding joy" (Jude 24).

10. Speak to yourselves - "Be filled with the Spirit; speaking to yourselves in psalms and hymns and spiritual songs, singing and making melody in your heart to the Lord" (Ephesians 5:18-19). Surprisingly, the Bible exhorts us to talk to ourselves; but when we are filled with the Spirit, the language will be in psalms, hymns, and spiritual songs. When we speak to ourselves in this manner, we will usually find that the Lord Himself will become a part of the conversation.

In conclusion: Paul exhorted the Corinthians to do some self-examination: "**Examine yourselves**, whether ye be in the faith;

prove your own **selves**" (2 Corinthians 13:5). If we will take heed to ourselves and save, delight and cleanse ourselves; and submit, humble and arm ourselves; and assemble, keep and speak to ourselves, then we will pass this "self" examination with flying colors!

PART II

IN THE BEGINNING GOD

A TALE OF TWO ADAMS

He wasn't sure exactly how or when it happened, but slowly the realization dawned—he was different from all the beautiful creatures that were slowly parading before him. As Adam continued naming them, one glaring difference stood out — they all had companions! He had none. He watched as they playfully nuzzled each other, snuggling and cuddling, and the awareness grew into an aching in his bosom. Something is missing! Lifting his head, Adam gazed expectantly down the long line. "Maybe my companion is in this line — perhaps this is the Lord God's unique way of introducing us," he thought hopefully. As the line dwindled, his diligent watch turned to a fervent search. At last, after naming the final stragglers, the conclusion was painfully obvious: he was alone — completely and miserably alone! He felt incomplete and the feeling was terribly painful.

"And the Lord God said, It is *not good* that the man should be alone" (Genesis 2:18, emphasis added). "And Adam gave names to all cattle, and to the fowl — and to every beast — but for Adam there was *not found* an help meet [suitable] for him" (Genesis 2:20, emphasis added). The words "not found" imply that Adam was indeed searching.

In chapter one, God "saw" six times that what He made "was good." At the end of day six, "And God saw every thing that he had made, and, behold, it was very [exceedingly] good" (Genesis 1:31). Then just eighteen verses later, in Genesis 2:18-20, we find *"not good" and "not found*!" It seems totally out of character for an omniscient, loving and good God to create something "not good" and "not found." What happened? Did God make a mistake? Of course not, God doesn't make mistakes! Then the only alternative was that He planned it this way.

And why did God tell His creation at the end of day six to be fruitful, and multiply, and then create Adam alone, all by himself? God could have simultaneously formed Eve from the dust of the ground right beside Adam! As a being created directly by God, Adam was uniquely called, "the son of God" in Luke 3:38. So, why did God subject this "son of God" to a painful scenario of loneliness, fervently searching and hoping for a companion, and then to a "deep sleep" and "rib surgery" to make the bride from his side? (See Genesis

2:21-22). We can be certain that the transcendent Creator of the cosmos had a plan, a definite reason, and everything was proceeding according to His Plan, which we may call the *logos*. The Bible is clearly the Answer Book showing us how all the pieces of the puzzle fit together. Let's humbly and prayerfully take a closer look.

The Clues

A fascinating clue to this enigma is found in 1 Corinthians 15:45 (emphasis added), "And so it is written, The *first man Adam* was made a living soul; the *last Adam* was made a quickening [life-giving] spirit..." (So, there *were* two Adams! And they were called, the first Adam and the last Adam!). "The first man is of the earth, earthy [made of dust]; the second man is the *Lord from heaven*" (Verse 47, emphasis added) So, Jesus is God!

Consider now a second clue which reveals an astonishing truth: as we look into the amazing parallels between the two Adams, we begin to realize that the first Adam was a *type* of the last Adam: Adam was a type of Christ! The apostle Paul expressly declared, "Nevertheless death reigned from Adam to Moses, even over those who had not sinned according to the likeness of the transgression of Adam who is a *type* of Him who was to come" (Romans 5:14, NKJV, emphasis added). The KJV agrees, rendering this phrase, "who is the *figure* of him that was to come." (emphasis added.) This fact will become even more apparent as we look briefly at some of the striking parallels between the two Adams. In summary: The first Adam was a type of the last Adam, Who, as the Lord from heaven, *formed* the first Adam from the dust of the earth! So, the last Adam created the first Adam to be a type of Himself and to play a role which He Himself was destined to fulfill! We sense a divine alignment with the two Adams.

The Parallels

Genesis 2:21-22: "And the Lord God caused a deep sleep to fall upon Adam, and he slept: and he took one of his ribs, and closed up the flesh instead thereof; and the rib... made he a woman, and brought her unto the man." In the Bible, death is often referred to as "sleep." For example, "Our friend Lazarus sleepeth; but I go, that I may awake him out of sleep" (John 11:11). Here, the first Adam's "deep sleep" was a perfect type and "shadow" of the deep sleep of death that Christ, the last Adam, suffered at Calvary. And when Jesus' side was pierced, a crimson stream of blood and water flowed out, thereby completing the redeeming of His Bride—the Church! Truly, the Bride of Christ was made from His side also.

Genesis 2:23: "And Adam said, This is now bone of my bones and flesh of my flesh." This unique phraseology is very similar to that used by Paul when speaking about Christ and the church, "For we are members of his body, of his flesh, and of his bones" (Ephesians 5:30). Picturing Adam's delight when he first met Eve, gives us an insight into why Jesus, "who for the joy that was set before him endured the cross" (Hebrews 12:2), was willing to suffer excruciating pain and agony, giving Himself for His Bride (See Ephesians 5:25).

The Leave, Cleave and Intimacy Parallels

Genesis 2:24 (emphasis added): "Therefore shall a man *leave* his father and his mother, and shall *cleave* unto his wife: and they shall be *one flesh*" This verse is the divine model for the institution of marriage and family. It contains three important keys:

1. "Leave" (Severance): though we are still commanded to honor our parents, we must leave them and, in essence, cut the cord. The last Adam, Christ, "the Lord from heaven," left the throne of glory, severing Himself from all of heaven's blessings and the adoration of angels.

2. "Cleave" (Permanence): we must cling to, hold fast to, adhere to, stick like glue to our companions. The espoused bride of Christ knows the permanence of "Lo, I am with you alway" (Matthew 28:20), "I will never leave thee nor forsake thee" (Hebrews 13:5), the cleaving principle of "neither shall any man pluck them out of my hand" (John 10:28), and nothing "... shall be able to separate us" (Romans 8:39).

3. "One Flesh" (Intimacy): The apostle Paul, in his Ephesians 5 discourse comparing the marriage relationship to that of Christ and the church, alludes to Genesis 2:24: "For this cause shall a man leave his father and mother, and shall be joined unto his wife, and they two shall be one flesh" (Ephesians 5:31). In the next verse, Paul reveals a surprising parallel with the last Adam, Christ: "This is a great mystery: but I speak concerning Christ and the church" (Ephesians 5:32)!

Genesis 2:25: "And they were both naked, the man and his wife, and were not ashamed." Surely, we will not dare offer this verse as a parallel to the last Adam. That would be sacrilegious. Yes, *Calvary* was sacrilegious in the extreme! "And when they had crucified him, they parted his garments, casting lots upon them, what every man should take" (Mark 15:24). There is debate about whether He wore a loin cloth, but even if He did, He was essentially naked. What about the words, "not ashamed"? "Looking unto Jesus ... who for the joy that was set before him endured the cross, *despising the shame* ..." (Hebrews 12:2, emphasis added). Not only was He "not ashamed," He *despised* the shame!

The Genesis 2:18-20 Parallels?

We just looked at the parallels in Genesis 2:21-25. Would it be asking too much to consider that the parallels actually began three verses earlier, encompassing Genesis 2:18-20? These verses portrayed the first Adam as alone, and it was "not good," and they also revealed his fervent, but fruitless, search for a companion who "was not found..." Knowing that the first Adam was a type of the last Adam, Who was "the Lord from Heaven" (1 Corinthians 15:47), would it be too much to consider that the first Adam was showing us that the Lord from heaven was alone, and it was "not good." And furthermore, that the Lord from heaven was desirous of a companion, a Bride, who "was not found." Following this typology shows how the Lord from heaven would acquire His Bride: she would be made from His side while He was in a "deep sleep" of death!

The Marriage!

Some may say, "This is just too far out. You're reading too much into this story of Adam and his portrayal, through typology, of a lonely God who wants to have a Bride." Well, if we fast forward to the end of the story, going to the back of the book, we will find that in Revelation 19, there will be a *marriage*! "Let us be glad and rejoice, and give honour to him: for the marriage of the Lamb is come, and his wife hath made herself ready. And to her was granted that she should be arrayed in fine linen, clean and white: for the fine linen is the righteousness of saints" (Revelation 19:7-8)!

So, *He ends up with a Bride*! Do you think this was just a

coincidence — just happenstance? Or was it His plan? Why would He want a wife? Do you think He might have been lonely, like He revealed through His prototype, the first Adam? This was His plan as shown in the book of Genesis, from the foundation of the world. Revelation 13:8 (emphasis added), declares: "... the *Lamb slain from the foundation of the world*." This verse proves conclusively that the plan was from the very beginning. "Thy word is true from the beginning" (Psalm 119:160).

The Plan

When the serpent deceived Adam and Eve in the Garden of Eden, then it became necessary for God to be manifest in the flesh (the Incarnation) to crush the serpent's head: "And without controversy great is the mystery of godliness: God was manifest in the flesh, justified in the Spirit, seen of angels, preached unto the Gentiles, believed on in the world, received up into glory" (1 Timothy 3:16 and see Genesis 3:15). The Incarnation happened in order for God to redeem His fallen creation and reconcile them back to Himself: "To wit, that God was in Christ, reconciling the world unto himself" (2 Corinthians 5:19)!

I Can Only Imagine

The WORD gets out: God is lonely and He wants a companion! The heavenly host recoils in disbelief: "But Lord, you've got us angels for friends, and now you have human beings, and you can walk with them in the garden. And they're going to be fruitful and multiply. That's wonderful. Surely that will provide enough companionship for you."

GOD: "Counsel with me here: my plan is to take these human beings, which, as you know, I made lower than you, and I'm going to elevate them to a higher plane. They are going to be my Bride!"

ANGELS: "Bride!? Why not just create a bride from nothing? Just speak her into existence."

GOD: "My Bride is going to be so SPECIAL! I will have to pay for Her! It's going to cost me... a lot...but She will be worth it!"

ANGELS: "How can this be?"

GOD: "Okay, here's a hint: It's a mystery: I'm going to become one of them. And it will cost me dearly." This proclamation is greeted with stunned silence!

ANGELS: "Why would you want to be one of them? How could you become one of them?"

GOD: "When it happens, you'll be the first to know. I'll let you herald the news."

Suddenly, one of the archangel's countenances darkened; the "anointed cherub that covereth" skulked away murmuring, "He's going to elevate His precious pets! What about me, I'm the one He should elevate! If I ever get the chance, I'll hit His precious pets so hard they won't know what hit them. He won't either. There will be no elevating them." Lucifer chanced to look back; the Lord was looking right at him, with an all-knowing grin on His face.

The Sin of the First Adam

Do we dare extend the parallels of the two Adams into Genesis 3 for the sin and consequent fall of the first Adam? An important clue to understanding the first Adam is found in 1 Timothy 2:14: "And Adam was not deceived, but the woman being deceived was in the transgression." Was Paul minimizing Adam's role in the fall? No, but since Adam was not deceived, we may be sure that he didn't nonchalantly eat the forbidden fruit. He must have knowingly chosen to share the death penalty with his bride. He was not deceived, but fully aware!

But why did Adam do this? What motivated him? Was it rebellion, or could he have been driven by his undying love for Eve? The Bible is silent concerning Adam's thought process leading up to his fateful decision. But it is not silent about the last Adam's thoughts and actions in fulfilling the typology. Here, we may gain tremendous insight into the first Adam's actions by applying the typology in reverse. We know the last Adam, Christ, fulfilled the role that was typecast for Him by the first Adam. We then extrapolate back to see the role that the first Adam *must have* played as a type for Him. We, thus, consider the parallels in reverse: we note what Christ did; then the first Adam must have done similarly, or he would not have been the *type of Him who was to come.*

We know the last Adam agonized in a garden — Gethsemane — concerning His role as a "Lamb slain" as a substitute death, being "made to be sin," and tasting death once for all: "And being in agony he prayed more earnestly: and his sweat was as it were great drops of blood" (Luke 22:44). We may be positively sure that Adam, as a type of Christ, must have greatly agonized in a garden also, the Garden of Eden, because disobedience, sin, and death were foreign and repulsive to him.

The Agony in Eden

It is highly possible, indeed probable, that the first Adam's prayer may have ascended to God as follows: "Dear Lord, you gave Eve to me to heal my loneliness. She is now part of me — bone of my bones and flesh of my flesh. Lord, you joined us together and now we are one; we are no longer two, but one. How, then, can I live separately from her? I have never disobeyed you; I know no sin, and I don't want to disobey you now. It's decision time. Oh Lord, I love you, I really do love you! You surely see my agony. Please understand me — I am not acting out of disobedience; but because my love for Eve is consuming me. For her sake, I am willing to become sinful — made to be sin. When you told me to *cleave* to her, I made up my mind to do just that. I determined to never let anything come between us or separate us. I don't know what this thing called death is, but since it's a penalty it must be horrible. If she has to leave me to suffer death, Lord, then I'm very sorry, but I will cleave to her in that also. So, I am choosing to suffer the penalty with her. My love for her will not die, so I'll have to."

And Christ did, in essence, fulfill the sin role, for it is written of the last Adam, "For he hath made him *to be sin* for us, [He] who knew no sin" (2 Corinthians 5:21, emphasis added). And, "The Lord hath laid on him the iniquity of us all" (Isaiah 53:6), and "... Who his own self bare our sins in his own body on the tree" (1 Peter 2:24).

Crunch Time

Being the perfect prototype that he was, it's highly conceivable that the first Adam prayed this prayer, as *crunch* time arrived: "Lord, if possible, let this cup pass from me; if not, would you please consider letting me die in Eve's place! Please let her live! She was deceived

Ron Schoolcraft

by the serpent! I love her! I can't bear to see her die. Please let me lay down my life as a ransom for my bride. Nevertheless, Lord, not my will, but your will be done."

What would the last Adam think of that prayer? Could that be a trace of a smile flickering across the face of God? "Well done, first Adam, you have displayed a sacrificial love worthy of our shared name. Now I, the last Adam, the Lord from heaven, must someday make the same agonizing choice for my bride that I love — the church!" *And He did!* "Husbands, love your wives, even as *Christ also loved the church, and gave himself for it*.... That he might present it to himself a glorious church..." (Ephesians 5:25-27, emphasis added).

It's important to note: when Jesus gave His life for His Bride, He didn't have a Bride YET! "... while we were yet sinners, Christ died for us" (Romans 5:8). In giving His life for His Bride, He CREATED Her, and brought her into existence!

Conclusion

"A Tale of Two Adams" may seem to some as "a tale that is told" (Psalm 90:9), or even a "fairy tale." Time will tell. Perhaps a better answer is yet forthcoming, and some day we will more fully understand why God created the first man Adam to be a type of the last Adam, Jesus Christ (with God Himself incarnate in Him as "the Lord from heaven"). We may more fully understand the reason why He created the first Adam with two existing conditions that were, by His own admission, not good. He made him: (1) alone, "not good" (Genesis 2:18), and (2) yearning for a companion, "not found" (Genesis 2:20). And we may know why it was necessary to make Adam's bride from his side in contradistinction to the way He created the companions of all the other "kinds" of creatures. Were all these marvelous happenings and parallels merely incredible coincidences, or were they additional, divinely designed "figures (types) of the true" (see Hebrews 9:24.)?

Time will tell. But until then, we can rejoice in knowing that the last Adam, Jesus Christ, did indeed love His Bride, and sacrifice His life for her as she was made from His side. And, as the Lamb of Revelation 19, He will enter a covenantal marriage relationship with His Bride! "Let us be glad and rejoice, and give honour to him: for the marriage of the Lamb is come, and his wife hath made herself ready" (Revelation 19:7).

80

What a thrill to know we are invited to the marriage supper of the Lamb! "And he saith unto me, Write, Blessed are they which are called unto the marriage supper of the Lamb" (Revelation 19:9). We will not be going as guests but as *participants*! We, as the church, the Bride of Christ, are getting married! "... and his wife hath made herself ready. And to her was granted that she should be arrayed in fine linen, clean and white: for the fine linen is the righteousness of saints (Revelation 19:7-8)! To God be the glory!

So, here is our takeaway, sons of Adam: "Husbands, love your wives, even as Christ also loved the church, and gave himself for it" (Ephesians 5:25). If husbands will learn loving and giving, that sacrificial love, as Christ did for the church, then wives will relate to their husbands as the church does to Christ, reverencing and living for Him. Wives will be esteeming their husbands as loving saviors and will be only too happy to reverence and live for them as the church does for Christ!

"Now unto him that is able to keep you from falling, and to present you faultless before the presence of his glory with exceeding joy, To the only wise God our Saviour, be glory and majesty, dominion and power, both now and ever. Amen" (Jude 24-25).

Ron Schoolcraft

ONENESS 101

Welcome to Oneness 101, an introductory level study of the basic facts and fundamentals of the "Oneness" teaching that remains one of the bulwarks of the Apostolic Pentecostal body of beliefs. This great truth of "The Mighty God in Christ" is one of the distinctive revelations, along with baptism in Jesus' Name, that separates us from other beliefs and prepares us to be ready for the Rapture of His Church.

Is Jesus in the Godhead?

The "Godhead" simply means the "Godhood," the essential being or nature of God. Many today believe the Godhead is comprised of God the Father, God the Son, and God the Holy Ghost. They are called three Persons, the Trinity, and are deemed to be separate and distinct, co-equal and co-eternal. This teaching states that Jesus is the 2nd Person in the Godhead. But the Bible clearly and succinctly declares that Jesus could not be the 2nd Person in the Godhead! Because in fact, *He is not even in the Godhead!*

It's All in Him!

Colossians 2:8-10 warns, "Beware lest any man spoil you through philosophy and vain deceit, after the tradition of men, after the rudiments of the world, and not after *Christ. For in him dwelleth all the fulness of the Godhead bodily.* And ye are complete in him...." (Emphasis added.)

Here is the most clearcut distinction in the Bible between trinity and oneness: the Godhead is in Jesus! Jesus is not the 2nd person in the Godhead. He is not even in the Godhead — it's in Him! If Paul had just said, "...for in him dwelleth the Godhead" it would have been enough to convey the meaning. But he doubled down on it with: "... the **fulness** of the Godhead..." The "fulness" means the totality, the full-orbed deity! But that's not all: Paul tripled down on it by saying:

"**all** the fulness"! The NIV rendering agrees: "For in Christ *all the fulness of the Deity* lives in bodily form." (Emphasis added.) Yes, the NIV declared "all the fulness of the Deity" also! The Bible can't get any clearer. Note the preceding verse, Verse 8, "Beware lest any man spoil you through philosophy...." To "spoil" means "takes you captive" (NIV). NKJV uses "cheat you."

So, any empty, deceptive philosophy teaching that all the fulness of the Godhead does not dwell in Jesus Christ bodily, is trying to take you captive, lead you away, spoil and cheat you. Beware!

Verse 10 reveals: "And ye are **complete in him**...." (Emphasis added.) Somehow, being *complete in Him* means so much more when we know *"all the fulness of the Godhead"* is *in Him*!

Back to the Basics

Deuteronomy 6:4-7 trumpets: "Hear, O Israel: The LORD our God is one LORD: And thou shalt love the LORD thy God with all thine heart, and with all thy soul, and with all thy might. And these words, which I command thee this day, shall be in thine heart: And thou shalt teach them diligently unto thy children...."

This passage is the definitive One God passage. It is called the *Shema* and is the bedrock foundation of our monotheistic beliefs. The *Shema*, Deuteronomy 6:4-7, had a noteworthy advocate in the New Testament.

Jesus Picks the Greatest Commandment

Mark 12:28-31 records, "And one of the scribes came, and ... asked him, Which is the first ["most important," NIV] commandment of all? And Jesus answered him, The first of all the commandments is, Hear, O Israel; The Lord our God is one Lord: And thou shalt love the Lord thy God with all thy heart, and with all thy soul, and with all thy mind, and with all thy strength: this is the first commandment. And the second is like, namely this, Thou shalt love thy neighbour as thyself. There is **none** other commandment **greater** than these" (emphasis added). The scribes were hoping Jesus would pick one of the Ten Commandments to goad Him into a debate. As usual, He outwitted them and, in the process, revealed the supreme importance of the Shema, which begins with, "Hear, O Israel; The Lord our God is one Lord." He concluded with, "There is none other commandment greater...."! This is heartening to know: it was not only the importance of our great love for God and our neighbor, but it was predicated on this proclamation: "The Lord our God is one Lord." He could have omitted it, but it was the integral foundation for the greatest commandment.

God Is a Spirit

John 4:24 declares, "God is a Spirit: and they that worship him must worship him in spirit and in truth." This is the basic definition of God: God is a Spirit, an invisible spirit. "... a spirit hath not flesh and bones, as ye see me have" Jesus explained to His disciples (Luke 24:39). This is a key to understanding the Godhead. God (Father) is a Spirit. God was made flesh (Son) at the Incarnation.

God Was Made Flesh

John 1:1 proclaims, "In the beginning was the Word, and the Word was with God, and the Word was God..." The Word (*logos*) was the plan, thought, mind, reason, the self-revelation of God, which was inseparable from God. The Word was God Himself! John 1:14 reveals: "And the Word was made flesh, and dwelt among us, (and we beheld his glory, the glory as of the only begotten of the Father,) full of grace and truth." So, God was made flesh, and thus, Jesus had a dual nature: that of humanity, as pertaining to His flesh, and of Deity (Divinity), as pertaining to the God incarnate in Him. The Deity is seen more clearly four verses earlier, in John 1:10: "He was in the world, and the world was made by him, and the world knew him not."

Jesus was truly unique. He was the God/man! He had a dual nature. "In Him Divinity and humanity were fused, not confused," as preeminent Oneness theologian Gordon Magee has stated. Since He had a dual nature, we should not think it strange that He played dual roles. At times He was portraying His humanity and at other times His Deity. As a man He became thirsty and drank water; as God He walked on water! He became hungry and ate bread and fish as a man; He multiplied the five loaves and two fishes to feed the five thousand as God! He cleansed and healed the lepers, opened blind eyes, raised the dead, forgave sins and received worship as God! He became weary, hungry, wept, suffered grief, sorrow, agony, and felt God-forsaken as man. And sometimes He played both roles simultaneously, as in John 3:13: "And no man hath ascended up to heaven, but he that came down from heaven, even the Son of man which is in heaven."

God Was Manifest in the Flesh

1 Timothy 3:16 reveals: "And without controversy great is the mystery of godliness: God was manifest in the flesh, justified in the Spirit, seen of angels, preached unto the Gentiles, believed on in the world, received up into glory." It was Jesus Christ Who was preached unto the Gentiles, believed on in the world, and received up into glory. So, this passage reveals that Jesus was a manifestation of God. God was manifest, made known, revealed in Jesus when the Word was made flesh. The Scriptures show that God has revealed Himself in three offices, roles, or manifestations: as the Father in Creation, the Son in Redemption, and the Holy Ghost in Regeneration. He was not three separate Gods or Persons but one God in three manifestations, roles, or offices.

We see an analogy of this in nature. The same cup of water in liquid form can be frozen into a solid form as ice or placed on a range and boiled, evaporating into the atmosphere as a gas. The same water appeared in three, completely different forms: liquid, solid, and gas.

This can also be analogous to one man who plays three completely different roles as a father, a son, and a husband. His wife, father, and son could write essays describing him in each of his roles that would make him seem as if he were three completely different people. But he is still one man playing three roles. In like manner, "The Lord our God is one Lord," and He has one name. (See Isaiah 9:6, Matthew 28:19, Acts 2:38 and Acts 4:12.)

Comparative Scriptures

A careful study of the Scriptures in the Old Testament which describe the attributes and identity of God, when compared with the Scriptures in the New Testament describing those same attributes and identity of Jesus Christ, will yield an astonishing conclusion: They are one and the same! The Lord God of the Old Testament is the Lord Jesus Christ of the New Testament! "The Lord our God is one Lord" (Deuteronomy 6:4)! (This study is based on the tract, "Wheel of Prophecy, Who Is God?" compiled by Pentecostal Pioneer, C.P. Kilgore.) We will study four categories: God the Creator, God the Savior, God the I AM, and I AM He, and God the First and Last.

God the Creator: Isaiah 44:24, "Thus saith the LORD, thy redeemer, and he that formed thee from the womb, I *am* the LORD that maketh all *things;* that stretcheth forth the heavens alone; that spreadeth abroad the earth by myself;"

Jesus the Creator: John 1:10 (Emphasis added), "He was in the world, and *the world was made by him,* and the world knew him not." Colossians 1:14-16 (emphasis added), "In whom we have redemption through his blood, *even* the forgiveness of sins: Who is *the image of the invisible God,* the firstborn of every creature: For by him were all things created, that are in heaven, and that are in earth, visible and invisible, whether *they be* thrones, or dominions, or principalities, or powers: *all things were created by him, and for him:*"

God the Savior: Isaiah 45:21, "Tell ye, and bring *them* near; yea, let them take counsel together: who hath declared this from ancient time? *who* hath told it from that time? *have* not I the LORD? and *there is* no God else beside me; a just God and a Saviour; *there is* none beside me." Luke 1:46, "And Mary said, My soul doth magnify the Lord, And my spirit hath rejoiced in God my Saviour."

Jesus the Savior: Luke 2:10-11, "And the angel said unto them, Fear not: for, behold, I bring you good tidings of great joy, which shall be to all people. For unto you is born this day in the city of David a Saviour, which is Christ the Lord." Titus 2:13, "Looking for that blessed hope, and the glorious appearing of the great God and our Saviour Jesus Christ;"

God the I AM: Exodus 3:13-14, "And Moses said unto God, Behold, *when* I come unto the children of Israel, and shall say unto them, The God of your fathers hath sent me unto you; and they shall say to me, What *is* his name? what shall I say unto them? And God said unto Moses, I AM THAT I AM: and he said, Thus shalt thou say unto the children of Israel, I AM hath sent me unto you."

Jesus the I AM: John 8:56-59, "Your father Abraham rejoiced to see my day: and he saw *it,* and was glad. Then said the Jews unto him, Thou art not yet fifty years old, and hast thou seen Abraham? Jesus said unto them, Verily, verily, I say unto you, Before Abraham was, I am. Then took they up stones to cast at him…" John 18:5-8, "They answered him, Jesus of Nazareth. Jesus saith unto them, I am *he.* And Judas also, which betrayed him, stood with them. As soon then as he had said unto them, I am *he,* they went backward, and fell to the ground… Jesus answered, I have told you that I am *he*…let these go their way." (Note: when Jesus said, "I am *he*", the word *he* is in italics. This means it was not in the original manuscripts. Thus, He said, "I am." He was claiming to be God, and this is why "they went backward and fell to the ground.") John 8:24, "I said therefore unto you, that ye shall die in your sins: for if ye believe not that **I am** *he,* ye shall die in your sins." John 8:27, "They understood not that he spake to them of the Father."

God the First and Last: Isaiah 44:6, "Thus saith the LORD the King of Israel, and his redeemer the LORD of hosts; I *am* the first, and I *am* the last; and beside me *there is* no God."

Jesus the First and Last: Revelation 1:17-18, "And when I saw him, I fell at his feet as dead. And he laid his right hand upon me, saying unto me, Fear not; I am the first and the last: *I am* he that liveth, and was dead; and, behold, I am alive for evermore,

Amen; and have the keys of hell and of death." Revelation 22:13 (Emphasis added), "I am Alpha and Omega, the beginning and the end, *the first and the last.* V. 16, *"I Jesus* have sent mine angel to testify unto you…"

Three Great Oneness Passages

John 14:7-10 (emphasis added): "If ye had known me, ye should have known my Father also: and from henceforth ye know him, and have seen him. Philip saith unto him, Lord, shew us the Father, and it sufficeth us. Jesus saith unto him, Have I been so long time with you, and yet hast thou not known me, Philip? *he that hath seen me hath seen the Father*; and how sayest thou *then,* Shew us the Father? … the Father that dwelleth in me, he doeth the works."

This is crystal clear. Many claim this is the passage that revealed Oneness to them. We cannot see the Father apart from Jesus. When we see Jesus, we see the Father. We can't see the Father outside of Jesus. Jesus taught in John 4:24, "God is a Spirit…" A spirit can't be seen. Jesus said, in Luke 24:39, "…for a spirit hath not flesh and bones, as ye see me have."

David Bernard posits an excellent illustration of this truth using an imaginary parallel scene in heaven. Paraphrasing: when we get to heaven, if someone were to say, "Great talking with you, Jesus. Could we talk with the Father? Where is the Father, could you show us the Father?" What would Jesus' answer be? Undoubtedly, He would say, "I was asked that question while on earth, by Phillip. My answer is still the same, because, "… my word is forever settled in heaven (Psalm 119:89). 'He that hath seen me hath seen the Father; and how sayest thou, then, shew us the Father'" (John 14:9)?

John 20:28,29 echoes, "And Thomas answered and said unto him, My Lord and my God. Jesus saith unto him, Thomas, because thou hast seen me, thou hast believed: blessed are they that have not seen, and yet have believed." Thomas had been doubting that Jesus had risen from the dead. When Jesus appeared to him, showed him His hands and side, and offered to let him touch His wounds, Thomas immediately became a believer in the Resurrection and the fact that Jesus was Lord and God. It is noteworthy that Jesus did not correct him but proclaimed a blessing on all that would believe without having to see it.

Matthew 28:19 commissions, "Go ye therefore, and teach all nations, baptizing them in the name of the Father, and of the Son, and of the Holy Ghost:" (Compare with Acts 2:38, Acts 8:16, Acts 10:48, Acts 19:5, and Acts 22:16.)

This marvelous Scripture just happens to be one of the most awesome and enlightening oneness passages in the Bible. Without Matthew 28:19 we would not know so precisely and absolutely that Jesus is the name (note: "name" is in the singular) of the Father, and of the Son, and of the Holy Ghost. The crystal-clear proof is found in the book of Acts where the apostles obeyed Matthew 28:19 by baptizing in the name of Jesus! (See Acts 2:38, 8:16, 10:48, 19:5 and 22:16.) This is the principle of biblical interpretation called, "The Harmony of the Scriptures." We know the Scriptures do not contradict or conflict, they harmonize. When we ask, "What is the name?" of the Father, Son, Holy Ghost, the only possible answer is, "JESUS!" This is confirmed by Acts 4:12, "Neither is there salvation in any other for there is none other name under heaven given among men whereby we must be saved." Matthew 28:19 proves there is just one name for this one God, and Acts confirms that it is Jesus!

Other principles of biblical interpretation that prove Jesus is the Name in Matthew 28:19: "Scripture interprets Scripture," and "Clear Scriptures interpret obscure and unclear Scriptures."

LORD, LIAR, OR LUNATIC

Noted Christian apologist, Josh McDowell, in his book, *EVIDENCE That Demands a VERDICT,* popularized the profound teaching of C.S. Lewis on the Deity of Christ. Lewis, a Cambridge professor and former agnostic, wrote in *Mere Christianity*, "I am trying here to prevent anyone saying the really foolish thing people often say about

Him (Jesus): 'I'm ready to accept Jesus as a great moral teacher, but I don't accept His claim to be God.' That is the one thing we must not say."[22] Lewis wrote that since Jesus clearly claimed to be God, if this were not true, then He could not be a great moral teacher but something much worse.

McDowell amplified Lewis: "Jesus claimed to be God... Jesus' claim to be God must be either TRUE or FALSE. (Two Alternatives)."

TRUE: He is LORD. (You can ACCEPT or REJECT.)

FALSE: (Two Alternatives)

1. He KNEW His Claims were FALSE; He made a deliberate misrepresentation: He was a LIAR.

2. He DID NOT KNOW His Claims were FALSE; He was sincerely deluded: He was a LUNATIC.

"The Trilemma --- Lord, Liar, or Lunatic?"

C.S. Lewis summarizes: "You can shut Him up for a fool, you can spit at Him and kill Him as a demon; or you can fall at His feet and call Him Lord and God. But let us not come up with any patronizing nonsense about His being a great human teacher. He has not left that open to us. He did not intend to." [23]

Josh McDowell summarizes: "The evidence is clearly in favor of Jesus as Lord ... There needs to be a moral honesty in the above consideration of Jesus as either a liar, lunatic or Lord and God."[24]

The Word of God summarizes: John 20:28,29, "And Thomas answered and said unto him, My Lord and my God. Jesus saith unto him, Thomas, because thou hast seen me, thou hast believed: blessed are they that have not seen, and yet have believed."

Let us fall at His feet and worship Him, "**Jesus, my Lord and my God!**"

DOWN FROM HIS GLORY

This marvelous Oneness truth is wonderfully expressed in the amazing anthem, "Down from His Glory," written by William E. Booth-Clibborn, in 1921.[25]

Down from His glory, ever living story,
My God and Savior came, and Jesus was His Name.
Born in a manger, To His own a stranger,
A man of sorrows, tears and agony.

Refrain:
O how I love Him! How I adore Him!
My breath, my sunshine, my all in all.
The great Creator became my Savior,
And all God's fulness dwelleth in Him.

What condescension, bringing us redemption;
That in the dead of night, Not one faint hope in sight,
God, gracious, tender, Laid aside His splendor,
Stooping to woo, to win, to save my soul.

Without reluctance, Flesh and blood His substance,
He took the form of man, Revealed the hidden plan,
O glorious myst'ry, Sacrifice of Calv'ry,
And now I know Thou art the great "I Am."

©1921 William E. Booth-Clibborn

EVOLUTION IN CRISIS?

Today's leading evolutionists are deeply divided over how evolution supposedly happens. Great Britain's prestigious Royal Society recently held a conference to deliberate if evolutionary theory needed to be extended, reformed, or totally overhauled to accommodate new ideas. [26]

In John Hands' report, "Is It Time to Drop Darwinism?" he described the current Neo-Darwinism model as a "statistical model validated not by observation or experiment, but by simplistic games models borrowed from 1940s economics."[27]

Attendee J. MacAllister summarized the sentiment of many, that the current model "is a misconception of reality that has reached the limits of its explanatory power. The problems are fundamental. No amount of cosmetic surgery is going to correct them."[28] Patrick Bateson of Cambridge, a fellow of this august body, stated flatly, "Natural Selection is not an agent."[29]

Definition of Evolution

By evolution we mean macroevolution, large scale evolution, from "molecules to man," "particles to people," which is what people usually mean when talking about evolution. It is the belief that life began by random chance in some primordial soup, and over millions of years slowly evolved from one-celled creatures into man. Or "from goo to you by way of the zoo."

Most know intuitively that man didn't come from animals, but, pressured by decades of brainwashing and intellectual blackmail (*all intelligent people believe evolution is a fact*), many mistakenly think there might be something to it. But there are thousands of advanced-degree scientists, members of several creation-science organizations, who don't believe in macroevolution.

Change Has Limits

Yes, there has been change down through history: fruit fly experiments showed that the flies' wings and eyes changed shape and color. But through countless mutations and generations they remained fruit flies. Darwin's finches showed variation in beaks, but they remained finches. There are always limits, or boundaries, to the variations, beyond which the changes cannot go. These genetic variations may yield differing varieties of roses or different breeds of dogs and cats, but the roses never turn into orchids, nor dogs into sheep, nor cats into squirrels. These limited genetic variations are then called by evolutionists, "*micro*evolution," and extrapolated to justify belief in "*macro*evolution." This is the old "bait and switch" ploy. But there is no evidence for macroevolution from modern science (observation, experimentation, repeatability, etc.), or from the fossil record. If macroevolution were true, the fossil record, with its billions of fossils, should be replete with intermediate, transitional (in-between) forms because life would have been in a continuous flux, changing from one kind of life to another. We should find fossils with legs changing into wings, half leg and half wing, and scales changing into feathers, and invertebrates starting to develop backbones. Instead, all we find are the ubiquitous gaps and "missing links."

Darwin even recognized this as "the most obvious and serious objection which can be urged against the theory."[30] He thought the fossils would eventually be found. Now, one hundred and sixty-plus years later, all we have is a handful of questionable fossils which not even all paleontologists agree on. This lack of transitional fossils is why Goldschmidt proposed his "hopeful monster" theory, and Stephen Jay Gould his "punctuated equilibrium" hypothesis. There is no evidence for either of them.

Are There Any Transitional Fossils?

Luther Sunderland interviewed five leading fossil experts from the world's major fossil museums for his book, *Darwin's Enigma: Fossils and Other Problems*.[31] None of the five museum officials could offer a single example of a transitional series of fossilized organisms that would document the transformation of one basically different type to another. Dr. Colin Patterson, a senior paleontologist at the British Museum of Natural History, spoke most freely about the absence of transitional forms. Patterson was asked by a reader why he didn't include a single photograph of a transitional fossil in his book, *Evolution*, (1978.) He replied on April 10, 1979, in a most candid letter: "I fully agree with your comments on the lack of direct illustration of evolutionary transitions in my book. If I knew of any, fossil or living, I would certainly have included them ... Gould and the American Museum people are hard to contradict when they say there are no transitional fossils ... I will lay it on the line — there is not one such fossil for which one could make a watertight argument ... Is Archaeopteryx the ancestor of all birds? Perhaps yes, perhaps no; there is no way of answering the question. It is easy enough to make up stories of how one form gave rise to another ... but such stories are not part of science, for there is no way of putting them to the test."[32]

Drs. David Raup and Steven Stanley have remarked, "Commonly new higher categories appear abruptly in the fossil record without evidence of transitional forms."[33] Stephen Jay Gould has stated, "The extreme rarity of transitional forms in the fossil record persists as the trade secret of paleontology ... a species does not arise gradually by the steady transformation of its ancestors; it appears all at once and fully formed."[34] This is why Gould proposed his "Punctuated Equilibrium" theory, that evolution has occurred in rapid bursts which left no evidence of gradual transitions. This sounds like the Genesis Creation account! These gaps and the lack of transitional fossils are the exact predictions of the Creation model of origins.

Return of the GOD Hypothesis

Dr. Stephen C. Meyer, Geophysicist, from Cambridge, has recently published, *Return of the GOD Hypothesis.* Meyer shows irrefutable scientific evidence pointing to God as the transcendent Creator of the universe. His subtitle: *"Three Scientific Discoveries That Reveal the Mind Behind the Universe."* The 3 discoveries: 1) The Universe had a beginning (as opposed to always existing eternally, as in the Steady State theory). 2) The universe has been finely tuned for life from the beginning. 3) The discovery of complex digital code (DNA) at the foundation of life. Meyer notes the inability of science to explain these discoveries on the basis of strictly materialistic hypotheses.[35]

On # 2, the fine-tuning of the universe: the fundamental laws and parameters of physics have precise numerical values. They could be set for any values, yet all these laws and constants conspire in a mathematically incredible way to make life in the universe possible. If they were off in the least, this universe and life could not exist. Parameters such as the expansion rate of the universe (the cosmological constant); if it were a little slower we would collapse into a black hole; a little faster, we would suffer a heat death; the location of the earth at just the right distance from the sun (a little closer, we burn up, a little farther away, we freeze); the force of gravity; earth's size, atmosphere, and many intricate cycles, such as the carbon, oxygen, and nitrogen cycles, etc., all are exquisitely fine-tuned. Some cosmologists have begun calling our universe the "goldilocks universe!" It takes an intelligent mind to fine-tune devices. Fine-tuning requires a Fine-tuner! A Creation requires a Creator!

Sir Fred Hoyle (who gave the Big Bang its name) was the first to discover a fine-tuning parameter: to build carbon in the universe, he found it necessary to build long, chain-like molecules. He commented, "A common sense interpretation of the facts suggests that a super-intellect has monkeyed with physics, as well as chemistry and biology, and that there are no blind forces worth speaking about in nature."[36]

Dr. Meyer had earlier written, *Signature in the Cell*, which showed an Intelligent Designer's autograph in every cell.[37] Dr. Meyer showed the incredible complexity of DNA, the double helix, jam-packed along the spine with coded information, and then looked at the mathematical probabilities, showing that chance evolution by random mutations acted on by natural selection was virtually impossible.

On # 3, the complexity of DNA: in recent years biologists have discovered an exquisite world of nanotechnology within living cells—complex circuits, sliding clamps, energy-generating turbines, and miniature machines. E.g. Bacterial cells are propelled by rotary engines called flagellar motors that rotate at 100,000 rpm. These engines look like they were designed by engineers, with many distinct mechanical parts (made of proteins), including rotors, stators, O-rings, bushings, U-joints, and drive shafts. Biochemist Michael Behe says the motor depends on the coordinated function of thirty protein parts.[38] Remove one and it doesn't work. Behe coined the term "irreducible complexity" to describe this phenomenon.[39] It can't function unless all thirty parts are present.

"INFORMATION: the Hallmark of the MIND"

To date, no theory of undirected chemical evolution has explained the origin of the digital information needed to build the first living cell. Why? There is simply too much information in the cell to be explained by chance alone. The God Hypothesis is based on scientific discoveries and our experience of cause and effect, the basis of all scientific reasoning about the past. We must follow the evidence where it leads!

Dr. Meyer was working with a Microsoft computer programmer, researching the unfathomable complexity of DNA. The MS programmer said, "I get a feeling somebody figured all this out before us, because I see all these computer design patterns, known ways of storing and processing information that we've recently developed in digital computing — present inside the cell."[40] These are indicators of a Master Programmer. Richard Dawkins, premier evolution spokesman from Oxford, said, "the machine code of the genes is uncannily computer-like."[41] Meyer quotes Bill Gates, "DNA is like a software program, only much more complex than anything we've ever devised."[42] Geneticist Francis Collins said DNA was "our own instruction book, previously known only to God."[43]

Meyer posits, there can be only one cause for the origin of information, whether found in a software program, an alphabetical text, imbedded in a radio signal, or a hieroglyphic inscription:

information in our experience always comes from a <u>mind</u>. (A super-intelligent, transcendent Mind!) Meyer said, "Information is the hallmark of the mind, and purely from the evidence of genetics and biology, we can infer the existence of a mind that's far greater than our own — a conscious, purposeful, rational, intelligent Designer who's amazingly creative."[44]

Some mainstream evolutionary biologists are now rejecting the neo-Darwinian model because the mutation/natural selection mechanism, in their own view, lacks creative power. They are now trying to explore, find, formulate, and await the discovery of new theories of evolution because of the inadequacy of the neo-Darwinian view.

Francis Collins — "Nature Points to God"

Collins is a renowned scientist and the director of the Human Genome Project. In his Veritas Forum speech at Caltech, explaining his journey from atheism to Christianity, he listed these interesting ways that nature points to God: "1) There is something instead of nothing — no reason that should be. 2) The unreasonable effectiveness of mathematics. It works *very well.* 3) The Big Bang: the universe had a beginning. It seems something came out of nothing. Nature does not allow that. Nature can't create itself. 4) The precise fine-tuning of the physical constants of the universe, a whole series of laws that govern the behavior of matter and energy; e.g. the gravitational constant. Our existence exists on the knife edge of improbability. Applying the principle of Occam's Razor: the simplest explanation is probably the correct one. 5) The Moral Law: there is something called right and something called wrong. We're supposed to do the right thing, not the wrong thing. It is interesting that the moral law is *written in our own hearts!*"[45]

Collins cited German philosopher Immanuel Kant: "Two things fill me with constantly increasing admiration, and awe, the longer and more earnestly I reflect on them: the starry heavens without and the moral law within."[46]

Lee Strobel — Science Pointed Him Back to God

Lee Strobel, in The *Case for Christianity Answer Book,* states, "Evolutionists accept by faith these misguided ideas: 1) Nothing produces everything (in the beginning there was nothing, it exploded, and now we have everything.) 2) Non-life produces life, 3) randomness produces finely-tuned design, 4) chaos produces information, 5) unconsciousness produces consciousness, and 6.) non-reason produces reason."[47] (It takes "blind faith" to believe any of these misguided ideas.) The likelihood that a living organism emerged by chance from a prebiotic soup is about as likely, according to astronomer, Fred Hoyle, as that a "tornado sweeping through a junkyard might assemble a Boeing 747 from the materials therein."[48] Or, we might add, that an explosion at the Seymour Tribune might produce a complete set of Encyclopedia Britannicas.

Strobel offers five questions evolutionists can't answer: 1) The formation of the universe itself (nothing exploded, where did all this matter, information, fine-tuning originate?) 2) The origin of the first life (the Law of Biogenesis says, life only comes from life.) 3) The encoding of complex information in DNA (where did all this coded information come from?) 4) The explosion of life in the Cambrian (the sudden appearance of a large multitude of complex life, multicellular life forms, invertebrate and vertebrate, in the fossil record, with no evidence of ancestors/precursors in the Precambrian rock layers.) 5) Systemic large gaps in the fossil record.[49] (The fossils still say no.)

Dr. Henry M. Morris, the "Father of Modern Creationism"

Dr. Henry Morris, in his study Bible, has said, 1) There is no present evolution. 2) There has been no past evolution (proven by the gaps in the fossil record.) 3) There can be no possible evolution: the universal laws of conservation and decay (I and II Laws of Thermodynamics) prohibit it. The direction of change is toward more randomness, disorder, downhill.[50] (Not uphill towards greater complexity.)

Jesus taught against false prophets and teachings, saying, "a corrupt tree bringeth forth evil fruit…by their fruits ye shall know them." (Matthew 7:16-20). Dr. Morris said, "The evolutionary philosophy has produced no good fruit whatsoever … it has generated atheism, humanism, communism, fascism, racism, and all manner of evil fruit. It, therefore, is a false and evil philosophy."[51] (It is well known that Hitler used evolution as his "scientific" rationale for genocide on the Jews. In the struggle for "survival of the fittest" they were no match for his "superior master race.")

Most don't know the complete title of Darwin's "Origin of the Species." Amazon.com shows twenty different books, but only one shows the complete title: *The Origin of Species by Means of Natural Selection Or the Preservation of Favoured Races in the Struggle for Life*." "*Favoured Races*!?" Who are the unfavored races who don't need preserving? His book will tell you.

Evolution and the Bible

Darwin and his theory of evolution did not catch God by surprise. **God Gave the Word** to forewarn us and prepare us to guard against this false teaching:

1 Timothy 6:20 (emphasis added) "O Timothy, keep that which is committed to thy trust, avoiding profane *and* vain babblings, and oppositions of *science falsely so called*:" There is knowledge that is falsely called science; it is in opposition to true science and is a false science. True science follows the steps of the scientific method and involves observation, experimentation, testing, repeatability, and falsifiability. The study of origins may be called historical science, but it is beyond the realm of true science because it is not subject to the steps of the scientific method for verification.

God Gave the Word of truth about the creation in Genesis, chapters 1 and 2. Other Scriptures confirm this, such as:

Hebrews 11:3 "Through faith we understand that the worlds were framed by the word of God, so that things which are seen were not made of things which do appear." God created "ex nihilo," out of nothing.

Ron Schoolcraft

Psalm 33:6-9 "By the word of the LORD were the heavens made; and all the host of them by the breath of his mouth. He gathereth the waters of the sea together as an heap ... For he spake, and it was done; he commanded, and it stood fast."

In an amazing passage, the Apostle Peter proclaims that last day scoffers (mockers) are willingly ignorant (they want to be ignorant) of three vitally important facts of the Scriptures: namely, 1) the Creation, by the Word of God, 2) the Worldwide Flood, and 3) the Coming Judgement:

2 Peter 3:3-12 (emphasis added) "Knowing this first, that there shall come in the last days scoffers [mockers], walking after their own lusts, And saying, Where is the promise of his coming? for since the fathers fell asleep, all things continue as they were from the beginning of the creation. For this they *willingly are ignorant of,* that *by the word of God* the *heavens were of old,* and the *earth standing out of the water and in the water*:[**the Creation**] Whereby *the world that then was, being overflowed with water, perished*:[**the Worldwide Flood**] But the heavens and the earth, which are now, by the *same word* are *kept in store, reserved unto fire against the day of judgment and perdition of ungodly men* [**the Coming Judgment**] .... But the day of the Lord will come as a thief in the night; in the which the *heavens shall pass away* with a *great noise* [a Big Bang], and the elements shall melt with fervent heat, the earth also and the works that are therein shall be burned up. Seeing then *that* all these things shall be dissolved, what manner of persons ought ye to be in all holy conversation and godliness, Looking for and hasting unto the coming of the day of God, wherein the heavens being on fire shall be dissolved, and the elements shall melt with fervent heat?"

The answer is to not be "willingly ignorant," but to be a willing believer, and join the believers in the promise of the next verse: 2 Peter 3:13, "Nevertheless we, according to his promise, look for new heavens and a new earth, wherein dwelleth righteousness."

2 Corinthians 10:4-5 (emphasis added) "(For the weapons of our warfare *are* not carnal, but mighty through God to the pulling down of strong holds;) *Casting down imaginations, and every high thing that exalteth itself against the knowledge of God,* and bringing into

captivity every thought to the obedience of Christ;"

These "imaginations," and "every high thing that exalts itself against the knowledge of God" are apt descriptions of evolutionist imaginations that exalt Mother Nature and Father Time as the creators of the universe and mankind, thus attempting to steal the glory from God, the true Creator.

The apostle Paul, in the first chapter of Romans, has some very somber warnings for those who change the truth of God into a lie, and worship and serve the creature (creation) more than the Creator:

"God Gave Them Up ... And Over"

Romans 1:20-32 (emphasis added) "For the invisible things of him from the creation of the world are *clearly seen*, being understood by the *things that are made, even his eternal power and Godhead*; so that *they are without excuse*: Because that, when they knew God, *they glorified him not as God*, neither were thankful; but became vain in their imaginations, and their foolish heart was darkened. *Professing themselves to be wise, they became fools*, And changed the glory of the uncorruptible God into an image made like to corruptible man, and to birds, and fourfooted beasts, and creeping things. Wherefore *God* also *gave them up* to *uncleanness* through the lusts of their own hearts, to dishonour their own bodies between themselves: Who *changed the truth of God into a lie*, and *worshipped and served the creature more than the Creator*, who is blessed for ever. Amen. For this cause *God gave them up unto vile affections*: for even their women did change the natural use into that which is against nature: And likewise also the men, leaving the natural use of the woman, burned in their lust one toward another; men with men working that which is unseemly, and receiving in themselves that recompence of their error which was meet. And even as *they did not like to retain God in their knowledge, God gave them over to a reprobate mind*, to do those things which are not convenient; Being filled with all unrighteousness, fornication, wickedness, covetousness, maliciousness; full of envy, murder, debate, deceit, malignity; whisperers, Backbiters, *haters of God*, despiteful, proud, boasters, inventors of evil things, disobedient to parents, Without understanding, covenant breakers, without natural affection, implacable, unmerciful: Who knowing the judgment of God, that they which commit such things are worthy of death, not only do the same, but have pleasure in them that do them."

Science is more and more pointing to God as the Transcendent Creator, Fine-tuner of the universe, and Savior of mankind! Evolutionists are twisting themselves into pretzels trying to get around the evidences for God. They are looking to the multiverse (multiple universe) theory for answers. That just begs the question, pushing it back one degree of separation without answering it. They would still need mechanisms to generate all these multiple universes, and they would each require the unexplained fine-tuning!

The OBSERVER!

Science does put a lot of stock in "observation," and rightly so. Amazingly, there was an Observer present in the beginning — the CREATOR! He not only inspired but *inscribed with His own finger* on tables of stone, as part of the 4th. Commandment, the Word of Truth about the Creation: "For in six days the LORD made heaven and earth, the sea, and all that in them is, and rested the seventh day: wherefore the LORD blessed the sabbath day, and hallowed it" (Exodus 20:11). And also, "It is a sign between me and the children of Israel for ever: for in six days the LORD made heaven and earth, and on the seventh day he rested, and was refreshed. And he gave unto Moses, when he had made an end of communing with him upon mount Sinai, *two* tables of testimony, *tables of stone, written with the finger of God*" (Exodus 31:17-18, emphasis added).

Yes, **God Gave the Word!** Let's take **His Word** for it, rather than the speculations of fallible men who doubt and question Him with "oppositions of science, falsely so called" (1 Timothy 6:20).

****

"Thou art worthy, O Lord, to receive glory and honour and power: for thou hast created all things, and for thy pleasure they are and were created" (Revelation. 4:11).

Revelation Song (Chorus)

"Holy, Holy, Holy is the Lord God Almighty, Who was, and is, and is to come,

With all Creation I sing: praise to the King of Kings! You are my everything, and I will adore You."[52]

Down from His Glory (Chorus)

"Oh, how I love Him, how I adore Him, my breath, my sunshine, my all-in-all!

The great Creator became my Savior, and all God's fulness dwelleth in Him!"[53]

Ron Schoolcraft

OLD TRAILS

Thus saith the Lord, Stand ye in the ways, and see, and ask for the old paths, where is the good way, and walk therein, and ye shall find rest for your souls.

Jeremiah 6:16

The twelve-year-old stripling mounted the bay, checked the calfskin waterbag slung to the back of his saddle, and rode out onto the rolling prairies of northern Colorado. It was the summer of 1911 and young Ralph Moody, also known as "Little Britches," was riding circuit as water boy on a large cattle ranch in the foothills of the Rockies.

When the herd grazed northward nearly to the Wyoming border, Ralph discovered a set of deep-worn old wagon wheel ruts. His curiosity aroused, he followed the overgrown trail for several miles, wondering: Why is it out here on the prairie, seemingly leading to nowhere? Who first broke this trail and why? So, Ralph asked the next man on his circuit, Hank Bevin, an old-time cowhand well into his sixties.

"What you stumbled onto was the trace of the old Overland Stagecoach Line," Hank answered. "I recollect when it run clean through from Missouri to Californy. Ben Holladay, he swung his stage line south'ard to pick up the Denver trade. This here's the way he went back north to get through the mountains."

"But how did he know where to get through the mountains?" Ralph asked.

"Old buffalo trails," said Hank. "Didn't ever you take note how the deepest buffalo and wild horse trails always leads by the easiest way to the nearest water, the best grass, and the lowest mountain passes? Remember that, if you aim to be a cattleman, and it'll save you a heap of trouble."

Ralph persisted. "I wonder how he happened to come through this way?"

"Didn't happen to — needed to," Hank replied. "Don't no man nor no wild critter wear a trail where he happens to go; only where he needs to go. It's all wrote down for them that can read, just like it is with a man. An old man's story is wrote in lines on his face; an old trail's story is wrote in lines on the earth's face."

This started Ralph Moody on a fascinating lifelong search for the origin and history of the ancient character lines that once seamed the face of the American West. His study culminated in his 1963 book, *The Old Trails West*.

Stay on the Trail

I was hooked. With Jeremiah's "old paths" prophecy ringing in my ears, I "hit the trail" myself, following trappers on the Old Spanish trail, traders and merchandisers on the Santa Fe Trail, and explorers Lewis and Clark on the Big Medicine Trail to the Columbia and Pacific. It seemed, as I journeyed, certain principles with spiritual applications leapt from the pages. They applied equally to mountain men and buffalo hunters on the Oregon Trail and settlers, gold rush parties, and Pony Express riders on the California Trail.

The best advice that could always be given was: stay on the established trails. Leave the old trails at your own risk. Those who attempted short cuts invariably had tragic endings with much loss of life and substance. Another trail tip: there was strength in unity and large numbers. Large caravans usually fared better than small, isolated groups, especially if attacked by Indians, because circling the wagons quickly proved advantageous. An isolated trail rider became an easy target. Perhaps a few examples will suffice.

Jedediah Smith

One of the most famous mountain men, the gifted explorer Jedediah Smith, discovered the overland route to California in 1826. In

1831 Jedediah led a caravan of twenty-three wagons loaded with trapper's supplies and trade goods out of Independence on the Santa Fe Trail. After crossing the Arkansas River near present Fort Dodge, he attempted a shortcut route at the Cimarron Cutoff. The flat, arid plain was void of any landmarks, and they became lost. Out of water, with mules dying by the score and men falling in their tracks, Jed Smith and Tom Fitzpatrick rode ahead to find the Cimarron River. Fitzpatrick's horse soon gave out, and Smith rode on alone. Isolated, he was no match for the small band of Comanches that surrounded him.

"There is a way that seemeth right unto a man, but the end thereof are the ways of death" (Proverbs 16:25). Is this shortcut, this new trail, plainly marked? David said, "Teach me thy way, O Lord, and lead me in a plain path, because of mine enemies" (Psalm 27:11).

Accurate trail maps were almost nonexistent. Tampering with trail markers and landmarks was a serious offense because it was a matter of life and death to stay on the trail. The Bible echoes this concern: "Remove not the old landmark" (Proverbs 23:10).

Another common mistake, especially among settlers, was overloading the wagons with too much excess baggage such as furniture, trunks of clothing, and elaborate camping equipment. The teams couldn't pull the heavy loads up the steep elevations, and much substance had to be jettisoned. This reminds us to be vigilant to "lay aside every weight, and the sin which doth so easily beset us" (Hebrews 12:1).

The Donner Tragedy

The most famous tragedy in American trail history was that of the eighty-seven member Donner party in 1846. The Donners gullibly followed the directions of a deceptive publication designed to divert thousands of settlers from Oregon to California. The author advised them to simply turn their wagons away from the Oregon Trail at Bridger's Fort, bearing west southwest, to the Salt Lake; and thence continue down to the Bay of San Francisco. It sounded so easy.

The Donners left Illinois in April 1846 at a plodding pace, assured that by taking the cutoff route they could easily reach San Francisco Bay by early fall. In spite of warnings by old-time frontiersman that the cutoff was impractical and dangerous, they continued their slow pace.

The party arrived at Bridger's Fort in now southwestern Wyoming on July 28, 1846. They left the Oregon Trail and set out to the southwest on an old trapper's trail. The trail soon entered a narrow canyon, impassable to wagons. In a panic, the men grabbed axes and crowbars and frantically hacked a roadway around the canyon. The Donner party fought its way through the Wasatch Mountains and reached Salt Lake in mid-September, completely disorganized.

They trudged across the Nevada deserts, losing much livestock to drought and Indian arrows. With winter approaching and provisions low they neared the Sierra Nevada Mountains. The Donner party reached the foot of the pass which would thereafter bear their name on the afternoon of November 3. By evening a howling blizzard was raging. It lasted several days, piling up three feet of snow, and when it ended, the party discovered that its cattle had drifted away.

Forty men, women, and children eventually lost their lives, and the gruesome story of the ensuing cannibalism is well known. The Donner party suffered an ordeal that is almost beyond belief, but it didn't have to be. They simply left an old established trail for an ill-advised short cut. Jeremiah's other warning about old paths seems noteworthy here: "Because My people have forgotten Me ... they have caused themselves to stumble in their ways, from the ancient paths, to walk in pathways and not on a highway" (Jeremiah 18:15, NKJV).

The Pony Express

In 1860 the Pony Express began offering ten-day mail service over the California Trail between St. Joseph and San Francisco. Four hundred fast horses and eighty courageous frontier riders were employed in relays along the nearly two thousand mile route. As the Civil War drew near in February,1861, Lincoln's inaugural address was deemed important to secure California's loyalty to the Union. The Pony Express prepared for a supreme effort to rush his message to Sacramento.

"Pony Bob" Haslam was chosen for the most hazardous relay — one hundred and twenty miles across western Nevada where the Paiute Indians, because of prior mistreatment, were on the rampage. The mail containing Lincoln's address reached Haslam soon after dawn, and within two minutes he was galloping westward. He was surprised when no Indians tried to ambush him in the two mountain passes. Pony Bob reasoned that they had probably set an ambush in the wide desert valley but circling it would cost three or four hours. Without hesitation he spurred straight down the trail, reins around the saddle horn and a pistol in each hand.

As Haslam feared, "war-painted Indians boiled out of the sagebrush like a pack of rabid wolves, and arrows filled the air like straws in a hurricane." He quickly broke through the main body of the pack only to find several warriors mounted on stolen Pony Express horses, too swift to outrun.

Haslam won through in a running battle of more than two miles, but an arrow ripped through his mouth, fracturing his jaw, and knocking out five teeth. Another lodged in his left arm at the shoulder. At the next relay station he stopped only to have the arrow cut out of his arm, and to mumble, "Fetch me a clean rag to hold in my mouth; I'm going on through."

His face was unrecognizable, his arm paralyzed and useless, but Pony Bob Haslam made it through, racing one hundred and twenty miles in eight hours, two minutes and twelve mount changes!

Apostolic Paths

At what peril do God's apostolic messengers descend into the valley of enemy territory — into a volley of hissing fiery darts from Satan? Some of these incendiary missiles may find their targets — only to be quenched by the shield of faith. The crucial need at this time is not only to fight the good fight but to "finish the course," to spur "straight down the trail" with "2:38's" blazing. When under heavy fire in enemy territory, it's not the time to seek a new trail or shortcut. We must stay on the old proven paths that were laid down by the Word of God and faithfully trod by the pioneers of our faith.

If we look closely, we can still see the traces of their deep-worn trails. These apostolic old paths are the surest way through these "rocky" mountains to the green pastures and refreshing waters of Home. To paraphrase old Hank, "Remember that, if you aim to be a Christian, and it'll save you a heap of trouble."

Are we still following the blessed old paths in personal devotion to prayer, fasting, and Bible reading? With evangelistic zeal in taking the message to unreached cities? And in perfecting holiness in the fear of God?

Hank said it well: "Don't no man nor no wild critter wear a trail where he happens to go; only where he needs to go." The historic "old paths" of the Bible and the apostolic faith were not laid down by happenstance or chance meandering; they were placed where God ordained them for our "needs." After all, "It's all wrote down for them that can read."

Happy Trails to You!
(Old trails, that is)!

From Mess to Messiah

The Trial of the Four

On the docket today are four ill-fated, Old Testament Gentile women. They are called "ill-fated" because they are women of "ill-fame," meaning that they are of questionable reputation. Some have labeled them as wicked, ungodly, and sinful. A courtroom trial by jury has been chosen to allow the Prosecuting Attorney to carefully present any incriminating evidence. Also, an Attorney for the Defense will represent the four defendants.

The jury is now seated, let the trial begin. The judge slams the gavel and announces that court is now in session, and we will now have brief opening statements from the attorneys, with the Prosecutor up first.

Prosecuting Attorney: "Your Honor, ladies and gentlemen of the jury, thank you for this honor. I will be brief. I am going to present irrefutable evidence of the guilt of these four women. I will be using only one exhibit for evidence: exhibit A is the Holy Bible, the sacred Scriptures. I perceive you are a God-fearing, Bible-believing people, and I trust you will be in one accord with the Word of God. In closing, I want to point out the audacity of these four women: they each, unbelievably, brought a date to these noble court proceedings! A date? Yes, a date! A *date with destiny*! Their destinies have finally caught up with them, and we shall soon see them found guilty ... with a penalty of death! Thank you, your Honor."

Defense Attorney: "Your Honor, ladies and gentlemen of the jury, I am pleased to represent these four women in court. This ill-fated foursome does, indeed, have a date with destiny. They will ultimately appear in the record, woven together in a tapestry far more beautiful than you or I, or even they themselves, could have ever imagined. Now, I am going to prophesy: someday in the far distant future, somewhere in a far-away land, someone will rise and call these four women, "Trophies of Grace!" I foresee that the Bible will give evidence to support this! Thank you, your Honor."

Judge: "Prosecuting Attorney, you may proceed with the prosecution of the first defendant."

Prosecuting Attorney: "Thank you, your Honor, Ladies and gentlemen of the jury. We will begin with exhibit A, the Bible, reading from Genesis 38:1-6. The first defendant is:"

1. Tamar

> And it came to pass at that time, that Judah went down from his brethren, and turned in to a certain Adullamite, whose name was Hirah. And Judah saw there a daughter of a certain Canaanite, whose name was Shuah; and he took her, and went in unto her. And she conceived, and bare a son; and he called his name Er. And she conceived again, and bare a son; and she called his name Onan. And she yet again conceived, and bare a son; and called his name Shelah: and he was at Chezib, when she bare him. And Judah took a wife for Er his firstborn, whose name was Tamar.
>
> Genesis 38:1-6

"So, Genesis 38 begins with Judah, the fourth son of Jacob, marrying a Canaanite woman. Later, he picked Tamar as a wife for his firstborn son, Er. But the Lord slew Er and also Judah's second son, Onan. Judah then promised Tamar his third son, Shelah, to be her husband when he was old enough to marry. But Judah failed to keep his promise, so Tamar decided to take matters into her own hands. Veiling her face as a temptress, she sat by the wayside and beguiled Judah.

"Here I must digress to offer an apology in advance to you, Your Honor, the Jury, guests of the court, and those who may read of these proceedings in the future. I will describe in some detail the height of the folly of these four women. Their vile deeds will seem depraved, salacious, and offensive, but it is necessary to use the Bible to illustrate the depth of their wickedness. They are not above the law. We now continue the narrative in Genesis 38, starting with verse 15 through verse 26.

"When Judah saw her, he thought her to be an harlot; because she had covered her face. And he turned unto her by the way, and said, Go to, I pray thee, let me come in unto thee; (for he knew not that she was his daughter in law.) And she said, What wilt thou give me, that thou mayest come in unto me? And he said, I will send thee a kid from the flock. And she said, Wilt thou give me a pledge, till thou send it? And he said, What pledge shall I give thee? And she said, Thy signet, and thy bracelets, and thy staff that is in thine hand. And he gave it her, and came in unto her, and she conceived by him. And she arose, and went away, and laid by her vail from her, and put on the garments of her widowhood. And Judah sent the kid by the hand of his friend the Adullamite, to receive his pledge from the woman's hand: but he found her not. Then he asked the men of that place, saying, Where is the harlot, that was openly by the way side? And they said, There was no harlot in this place. And he returned to Judah, and said, I cannot find her; and also the men of the place said, that there was no harlot in this place. And Judah said, Let her take it to her, lest we be shamed: behold, I sent this kid, and thou hast not found her. And it came to pass about three months after, that it was told Judah, saying, Tamar thy daughter in law hath played the harlot; and also, behold, she is with child by whoredom. And Judah said, Bring her forth, and let her be burnt. When she was brought forth, she sent to her father in law, saying, By the man, whose these are, am I with child: and she said, Discern, I pray thee, whose are these, the signet, and bracelets, and staff. And Judah acknowledged them, and said, She hath been more righteous than I; because that I gave her not to Shelah my son. And he knew her again no more" (Genesis 38:15-26).

"So, Judah confessed, and the sad chapter concludes with the birth of Judah and Tamar's twin sons, Pharez and Zarah. Judah and Tamar never married. So, here we have a Canaanite outcast, Tamar, and her twins Pharez and Zarah. Tamar is obviously guilty on four counts: prostitution, fornication, adultery, and incest. What were you thinking, *Tammy?!* Judah was your father-in-law! The penalty for any one of these counts is death. I'm positive the jury will have no problem finding you guilty as charged."

2. Rahab

"Turning to the Bible again for evidence, we will read Joshua 2:1, And Joshua the son of Nun sent out two men to spy secretly, saying, Go view the land, even Jericho. And they went, and came into an harlot's house, named Rahab, and lodged there.

"What was God doing directing Joshua's two spies to find lodging in Jericho at a house of ill fame? To Rahab's credit she hid the two spies in stalks of flax on her roof and dispatched the king's men on a wild and futile chase. Rahab then bargained for her life, realizing that Jericho was doomed, since God was with Israel. The two spies had compassion for her and gave her a true token, the scarlet thread, which gave her a little hope. This hope notwithstanding, she cannot escape the label of harlot, and she cannot escape the death penalty awaiting her for her date with destiny.

"I'm sorry your Honor, I'm not defaming Rahab, I'm merely quoting Scripture which calls her a harlot at almost every mention of her name. I'm sure you, the jury, will follow the leading of the Scripture, and do your job in finding her guilty. I'm sorry, *Ray*-hab, you could have been a *ray* of hope, a *ray* of light for your friends and neighbors, but instead you foolishly chose the pleasures of sin and proceeded to make a mess of your life. And that is one thing you four have in common: you each made an absolute mess of your lives. I see nothing of any redeeming value left in any of your lives."

3. Ruth

"In building our case against Ruth, we will begin reading Ruth 1:1-4: Now it came to pass in the days when the judges ruled, that there was a famine in the land. And a certain man of Bethlehemjudah went to sojourn in the country of Moab, he, and his wife, and his two sons. And the name of the man was Elimelech, and the name of his wife Naomi, and the name of his two sons Mahlon and Chilion, Ephrathites of Bethlehemjudah. And they came into the country of Moab, and continued there. And Elimelech Naomi's husband died; and she was left, and her two sons. And they took them wives of the women of Moab; the name of the one was Orpah, and the name of the other Ruth: and they dwelled there about ten years" (Ruth 1:1-4).

"It's true, the reputation of Ruth was not as soiled as the other women under indictment, but she also hailed from a pagan background, being a Moabitess. The Moabites were the perpetual enemies of Israel. They were descendants of Lot and had become so wicked that they had been banned from 'the congregation of the Lord; even to their tenth generation. Deuteronomy 23:3,4 declares, 'An Ammonite or Moabite shall not enter into the congregation of the LORD; even to their tenth generation shall they not enter into the congregation of the LORD for ever: Because they met you not with bread and with water in the way, when ye came forth out of Egypt; and because they hired against thee Balaam the son of Beor of Pethor of Mesopotamia, to curse thee. Yes, it was the Moabites who hired Balaam to curse Israel (Numbers 22).' When that failed, the daughters of Moab entered the camp and seduced the Israelite men. Numbers 25:1, And the people began to commit whoredom with the daughters of Moab. The result: a plague that destroyed twenty-four thousand men (Numbers 25:1-9). To be called a 'Moabitess' was a horrible expression of contempt.

"Furthermore, God was *against* Naomi, and, by extension, Ruth. Listen to Naomi's testimony, 'Nay, my daughters; for it grieveth me much for your sakes that the hand of the LORD is gone out against me' (Ruth 1:13). Naomi's testimony continues in Ruth 1:20,21 'And she said unto them, Call me not Naomi, call me Mara: for the Almighty hath dealt very bitterly with me. I went out full, and the LORD hath brought me home again empty: why then call ye me Naomi, seeing the LORD hath testified against me, and the Almighty hath afflicted me'?

"What further need have we of witnesses?! Ladies and gentlemen of the jury, if we could call God to this witness stand, the Bible says He would *testify against* Naomi! Your Honor, the defense attorney is objecting that Ruth is not Naomi. But we all know that 'Ruth clave unto [Naomi]' (Ruth 1:14), and said to her, 'thy people shall be my people, and thy God my God' (Ruth 1:16). They were like two peas in a pod. This is known as *guilt by association!* If *God testifies against* them, how can the jury acquit? Ruth is a Moabitess, a daughter of Moab, whose women caused the deaths of 24,000 Israelites! If she had been old enough, she would have been one of the seducers. I'm sorry, Ruthie the Moabitess, but your date with destiny has finally arrived."

4. Bathsheba

"Your Honor, and ladies and gentlemen of the jury: of course, David was partly to blame for the sinful affair with Bathsheba. But she was probably not completely guiltless and was very likely complicit since she likewise suffered in sorrow the penalty of the death of their first child (2 Samuel 12:24). She was a Gentile by marriage to Uriah the Hittite and was probably influenced by Hittite idol worship and the immoral Hittite culture. Tell me, Bathsheba, did you think that because your name began with the word *Bath*, this gave you license to bathe in public? You knew that handsome King David, the giant killer, lived in the adjacent, royal palace overlooking your home. Did you not see him walking on his balcony occasionally? .... Your silence is deafening.

"Your Honor, let me tell you about these Hittites. The Hittites were descendants of Ham though Canaan's second son, Heth. Their moral depravity is illustrated by the fact that when Esau married two Hittite women, they 'were a grief of mind unto Isaac and to Rebekah' (Genesis 26:35). Rebekah suffered severe distress: 'I am weary of my life because of the daughters of Heth … what good shall my life do me?' (Genesis 27:46). Ezekiel explained the immorality of the kingdom of Judah thus: 'Your mother was an Hittite, and your father an Amorite' (Ezekiel 16:45).

"It is interesting to note that, even after David married Bathsheba, the Bible still often referred to her as the wife of Uriah: 'And the Lord struck the child that Uriah's wife bare unto David' (2 Samuel 12:15). It does seem that God did not recognize the legitimacy of her marriage. Furthermore, the prophet Nathan prophesied: 'Now therefore the sword shall never depart from thine house' (2 Samuel 12:10).

"There was a lot of death coming to the house of David. And it came! Your Honor, and ladies and gentlemen of the jury, may I submit for your consideration: the sword has not yet departed from David's house. The sword needs to be unsheathed for one more death! Bathsheba nearly destroyed David; she nearly destroyed the

Kingdom of Israel! Bathsheba committed adultery with the King of Israel, and she is guilty as charged. Wife of Uriah, **Bath**sheba, you were not worthy to be called David's wife, but you are worthy for the sword of death to be unsheathed and brandished for one more death!"

The Prosecution Rests

"Your Honor, and ladies and gentlemen of the jury, I have proved beyond doubt, beyond any reasonable doubt, using the Bible as irrefutable evidence, that these four women, Tamar, Rahab, Ruth, and Bathsheba are guilty as charged, and I recommend the death penalty for each of them. They made an absolute mess of their lives, and now must prepare to meet their Maker. I see nothing here to redeem. I trust you will not go against God and the Bible but you will find them guilty as charged. The Prosecution rests."

Judge

"Thank you, Attorney for the Prosecution. We are ready now for the case for the defense of these four women. Will the Attorney for the Defense rise and begin his presentation?"

Attorney for the Defense

"Yes, thank you, Your Honor, and ladies and gentlemen of the jury. I would like to say, for the record, the Defense *rests* also!"

Judge

"What?! You have not presented a case for your four defendants! You can't rest a case that has not been made. This is unheard of in the history of Jurisprudence! They will most certainly be found guilty without a case being made for their defense."

Attorney for the Defense

"Yes, your Honor, I understand. But the Defense *rests* on the *Mercy* and the *Grace* of *God*! Shall not the Judge of all the earth do right?"

The courtroom, as well as the judge, all sit in shocked, stunned disbelief. Everyone wants to talk at once, but the judge orders silence. The judge finally shrugs his shoulders and dismisses the jury for deliberations, knowing full well they will return with a verdict very quickly.

****

The jury soon returns displaying sullen faces and drooped shoulders. A heavy silence blankets the courtroom. The ill-fated four stand, guilt-ridden, with heads bowed.

The Verdict

The judge asks if a verdict has been reached. Yes, it is ready. The foreman of the jury rises to read the verdict: "Yes, Your Honor. We, the jury, in strict accordance with the Law of Moses, the Ten Commandments, and God's Sacred Word, do hereby find the four defendants, Tamar, Rahab. Ruth and Bathsheba, each guil ..." But wait! **Now, for...**

The Rest of the Story

Judge! What are you doing? What is happening here? The judge is stepping down from the bench! He approaches the hapless four. In a gesture of reconciliation, he extends his hands, palms upward. But something is wrong — horribly wrong! There on his palms is something red — those deep gouges — it's blood!

"My daughters, I have paid the penalty for your sins; your sins are forgiven!" the Judge announces. "Hide yourselves in My love. I love you. I have need of you. I have chosen you and I'm going to use you, all four of you. Now go in peace. Sin no more." The scene is beginning to fade. But the forgiven four are not going anywhere; they are staying. It looks like they are weeping, falling prostrate at His feet, sobbing profusely. Everything is getting hazy, misty, like a cloud of Shekinah Glory. A perfume of divine anointing is filling the room as the four let their incense rise, a sweet-smelling savor to God!

****

From Mess to Messiah

The mist is lifting. Where are we now? The sweet perfume of divine anointing permeates this room also. We feel the presence of God. A young man is bent over a scroll, writing intently with a fervency in his countenance. This looks like Matthew, the tax collector, one of Jesus' Twelve Apostles. Perhaps we may just peer over his shoulder ....

> The book of the **genealogy of Jesus Christ**, the Son of David, the Son of Abraham: Abraham begot Isaac, Isaac begot Jacob, and Jacob begot Judah and his brothers. Judah begot Perez and Zerah [the twins] by **Tamar**, Perez begot Hezron ... Salmon begot Boaz by **Rahab**, Boaz begot Obed by **Ruth**, Obed begot Jesse, And Jesse begot David the king. David the king begot Solomon by **her who had been the wife of Uriah**...And Jacob begot Joseph the husband of Mary, of whom was born **Jesus** who is called **Christ**"
>
> Matthew 1:1-6,16, NKJV, emphasis added

Oh, the Grace of God!

Yes, all four Gentile women, Tamar, Rahab, Ruth, and Bathsheba, are *included* and *mentioned together* in the *royal lineage of Jesus Christ*! They were woven together in a tapestry far more beautiful than they could ever have imagined! It is almost beyond belief to consider that God would breathe on Matthew to name these four women — and only these four — in the lineage of Christ! Such godly women as Sarah and Rebekah are not even mentioned in this genealogical list.

Trophies of Grace

These four women already had one strike against them by being Gentiles. The second strike was their pagan background in idol worship. Strike three (for three of them) was their sinful behavior, which was worthy of death under the law. And Ruth, being a Moabitess, was banned from the congregation of the Lord. But they did not strike out, because they turned to the God of Israel for redemption. They hit grand slam home runs! By including them in the genealogy of Christ, He made them special examples of His absolutely awesome and amazing grace. They were special

"Trophies of Grace."

Who among us has not had times when we felt our lives were an absolute mess, hopeless and irredeemable. Let's take a cue from the "Trophies of Grace," and let our "Mess" lead us to our "Messiah," the Lord Jesus Christ! If we will turn our hearts and lives to Him and hide in His Love, His Mercy, and His Grace, He will make a way where there seems no way, because He is the Way, the Truth, and the Life! Just like He did for the "Trophies of Grace." So be of good cheer and take courage. Let's let our Mess lead us to our Messiah!

"Find Grace"

"Let us therefore come boldly unto the throne of grace, that we may obtain mercy, and **find grace** to help in time of need" (Hebrews 4:16). With the excellent example given to us by the "Trophies of Grace," we should be encouraged to come boldly to the Messiah's throne of grace, where we shall find grace and mercy both. GRACE is an acronym for: "God's Riches At Christ's Expense!" Jesus has already paid the horrible price for us to receive God's riches! So, let's come boldly to His throne and "Find Grace!"

Ron Schoolcraft

A Tale of Two Great Mysteries
A Sequel to "A Tale of Two Adams"

The word "mystery" is found twenty-two times in the Bible. Its plural, "mysteries," is used five times. It is noteworthy that the Bible only recognizes two "great" mysteries. So, although there are many mysteries recorded in the Scriptures, only two times is the adjective "great" combined with the word "mystery." It may be even more significant, in fact amazing, that these two great mysteries appear to be connected, inextricably linked together, in a sublimely marvelous way that portends well for our eternal welfare, joy, and bliss with the only wise God our Savior, the Lord Jesus Christ.

As was noted in "A Tale of Two Adams," there were two Adams, the first Adam and the last Adam. (1 Corinthians 15:45). Paul expressly declared that the first Adam was a type of the last Adam (Romans 5:14, NKJV. KJV used "figure"). And the last Adam, Christ, was "the Lord from heaven" (See 1 Corinthians 15:47). The amazing parallels between the two Adams were noted, especially the deep sleep (of death for Christ) and the brides made from their sides (See John 19:34). Also noted were their agonizing prayers in the gardens: Gethsemane and Eden (Adam's agony in Eden was assumed by applying the typology in reverse.)

Great Mystery # 1

"And without controversy *great is the mystery* of godliness: God was manifest in the flesh, justified in the Spirit, seen of angels, preached unto the Gentiles, believed on in the world, received up into glory" (1 Timothy 3:16, emphasis added). The apostle Paul clearly taught that God was manifest (revealed) in the flesh, as Jesus Christ. The apostle John agreed in the first chapter of his gospel: "In the beginning was the Word, and the Word was with God, and the Word was God.... And the Word was made flesh, and dwelt among us, (and we beheld his glory, the glory as of the only begotten of the Father,) full of grace and truth" (John 1:1,14). The Word, which was clearly God in verse 1, was made flesh (Jesus Christ) in verse 14. John 1:10 further confirms: "He was in the world, and the world was made by him, and the world knew him not." 2 Corinthians 5:19 proclaims: "To wit, that God was in Christ, reconciling the world unto himself..." The crystal-clear truth of **Great Mystery # 1** is:

He Became One of Us!

Great Mystery # 2

"For this cause shall a man leave his father and mother, and shall be joined unto his wife, and they two shall be one flesh. This is a ***great mystery***: but I speak concerning Christ and the church (Ephesians 5:31-32, emphasis added). In this passage Paul summarizes his Ephesians 5 discourse comparing the husband/wife relationship to that of Christ and the church. He quotes Genesis 2:24 concerning the intimacy of marriage, and then declares it a *great mystery*, for he's not just speaking about the husband-and-wife relationship, but of Christ and the church! The crystal-clear truth of **Great Mystery # 2** is:

We Will Be One with Him!

No Longer Two

May I submit for your consideration: these two great mysteries are connected. They are linked together. They are not two but one! So how could the two great mysteries be divinely aligned into one? You already know. It was His plan from the beginning! He was "the Lamb slain from the foundation of the world" (Revelation 13:8). He purposefully became one of us so He could redeem us and purchase a Church/Bride for Himself, "That he might present it to himself a glorious church, not having spot, or wrinkle..." (Ephesians 5:27). "Let us be glad and rejoice, and give honour to him: for the marriage of the Lamb is come, and his wife hath made herself ready. And to her was granted that she should be arrayed in fine linen, clean and white: for the fine linen is the righteousness of saints" (Revelation 19:7-8).

He Became One of Us (1 Timothy 3:16)

SO

We Could Be One with Him (Ephesians 5:31-32)!

It is interesting to note that the word "alleluia" (hallelujah) is used only four times in the KJV Bible! And all four times are, appropriately, in the context of the victorious return of Christ and the marriage of the Lamb!

"And after these things I heard a great voice of much people in heaven, saying, *Alleluia*; Salvation, and glory, and honour, and power, unto the Lord our God ... And again they said, *Alleluia*... And the four and twenty elders and the four beasts fell down and worshipped God that sat on the throne, saying, Amen; *Alleluia*....And I heard as it were the voice of a great multitude, and as the voice of many waters, and as the voice of mighty thunderings, saying, *Alleluia*: for the Lord God omnipotent reigneth. Let us be glad and rejoice, and give honour to him: for the *marriage of the Lamb is come, and his wife hath made herself ready. And to her was granted that she should be arrayed in fine linen, clean and white: for the fine linen is the righteousness of saints.* And he saith unto me, Write, Blessed are they which are called unto the *marriage supper of the Lamb"* (Revelation 19:1-9, emphasis added)!

The conclusion is inescapable: we, as the church, are, in some unique, mysterious way, going to be united with the Lord Jesus Christ! One thing is for certain: we will no longer be looking through a glass darkly! Our vision will be crystal-clear, and we will know precisely as we are known. At present our finite minds cannot begin to comprehend the sheer, transcendent joy and ecstasy that await us. It is enough for now for us to know that the two great mysteries reveal one great truth! He planned it that way!

He Became One of Us

SO

We Could Be One with Him!

PART III

PSALMS ALIVE

SOLACE FROM THE PSALMS
IN THE TIME OF TROUBLE

Psa 27:5 For in the time of trouble he shall hide me in his pavilion: in the secret of his tabernacle shall he hide me; he shall set me up upon a rock.

Psa 9:9,10 The LORD also will be a refuge for the oppressed, a refuge in times of trouble. And they that know thy name will put their trust in thee: for thou, LORD, hast not forsaken them that seek thee.

Psa 9:13 Have mercy upon me, O LORD; consider my trouble which I suffer of them that hate me, thou that liftest me up from the gates of death:

Psa 20:1,2 The LORD hear thee in the day of trouble; the name of the God of Jacob defend thee; Send thee help from the sanctuary, and strengthen thee out of Zion;

Psa 31:7,8 I will be glad and rejoice in thy mercy: for thou hast considered my trouble; thou hast known my soul in adversities; And hast not shut me up into the hand of the enemy: thou hast set my feet in a large room.

Psa 32:7 Thou art my hiding place; thou shalt preserve me from trouble; thou shalt compass me about with songs of deliverance. Selah.

Psa 34:17-19 The righteous cry, and the LORD heareth, and delivereth them out of all their troubles. The LORD is nigh unto them that are of a broken heart; and saveth such as be of a contrite spirit. Many are the afflictions of the righteous: but the LORD delivereth him out of them all.

Psa 37:39,40 But the salvation of the righteous is of the LORD: he is their strength in the time of trouble. And the LORD shall help them, and deliver them: he shall deliver them from the wicked, and save them, because they trust in him.

Psa 41:1-3 Blessed is he that considereth the poor: the LORD will deliver him in time of trouble. The LORD will preserve him, and keep him alive; and he shall be blessed upon the earth: and thou wilt not deliver him unto the will of his enemies. The LORD will strengthen him upon the bed of languishing: thou wilt make all his bed in his sickness.

Psa 46:1,2 God is our refuge and strength, a very [intensively] present help in trouble. Therefore will not we fear ...

Psa 50:14,15 Offer unto God thanksgiving; and pay thy vows unto the most High: And call upon me in the day of trouble: I will deliver thee, and thou shalt glorify me.

Psa 54:6,7 I will praise thy name, O LORD; for it is good. For he hath delivered me out of all trouble.

Psa 55:17,18 Evening, and morning, and at noon, will I pray, and cry aloud: and he shall hear my voice. He hath delivered my soul in peace from the battle that was against me:

Psa 57:1-3 Be merciful unto me, O God, be merciful unto me: for my soul trusteth in thee: yea, in the shadow of thy wings will I make my refuge, until these calamities be overpast. I will cry unto God most high; unto God that performeth all things for me. He shall send from heaven, and save me from the reproach of him that would swallow me up. Selah.

Psa 59:16 But I will sing of thy power; yea, I will sing aloud of thy mercy in the morning: for thou hast been my defence and refuge in the day of my trouble.

Psa 61:1-3 Hear my cry, O God; attend unto my prayer. From the end of the earth will I cry unto thee, when my heart is overwhelmed: lead me to the rock that is higher than I. For thou hast been a shelter for me, and a strong tower...

Psa 71:20,21 Thou, which hast shewed me great and sore troubles, shalt quicken me again...and comfort me on every side.

Psa 77:10 And I said, This is my infirmity: but I will remember the years of the right hand of the most High.

Psa 91:15,16 He shall call upon me, and I will answer him: I will be with him in trouble; I will deliver him, and honour him. With long life will I satisfy him, and shew him my salvation.

Psa 107:28-30 Then they cry unto the LORD in their trouble, and he bringeth them out of their distresses. He maketh the storm a calm, so that the waves thereof are still. Then are they glad ... so he bringeth them unto their desired haven.

Psa 119:143 Trouble and anguish have taken hold on me: yet thy commandments are my delights.

Psa 138:7 Though I walk in the midst of trouble, thou wilt revive me....

Ron Schoolcraft

Psalm 27 — The Hide and Seek Psalm

During his years of running from King Saul, David had many hiding places. But one by one, each in turn, those hideouts were discovered and overrun by King Saul and his soldiers. Finally, David thought he had found a safe home among his enemies: King Achish. The king even gave David the town of Ziklag to live in. But while David and his men were away, marching to battle, Amalekite raiders destroyed Ziklag, burned it to the ground, and captured their wives and children. This was one of the lowest points in David's life. His men all lifted up their voices and wept, "until they had no more power to weep." They were even threatening to stone him! David had to encourage himself in the Lord his God. They were eventually able to recover all and defeat the raiders. (See 1 Samuel 30:1-19).

In the physical realm David never managed to find the perfect hiding place. But in the spiritual, he learned that the ultimate sanctuary, the safest place to hide, was in the Lord and His House! He certainly had this in mind when he wrote Psalm 27.

Psalm 27:1 "The LORD *is* my light and my salvation; whom shall I fear? the LORD *is* the strength of my life; of whom shall I be afraid?" (God's first spoken words were, "Let there be light!" (Genesis 1:3). He said, "I am the Light of the world" (John 8:12), and His Word is "a lamp unto my feet, and a light unto my path" (Psalm 119:105); "...the joy of the Lord is your strength" (Nehemiah 8:10). But sometimes we must wait for that strength: "They that wait upon the Lord shall renew their strength" (Isaiah 40: 31).

Psalm 27:3 "Though an host should encamp against me, my heart shall not fear: though war should rise against me, in this *will* I *be* confident." (God knows a thing or two about camping!) "The angel of the Lord encampeth round about them that fear him, and delivereth them" (Psalm 34:7).

Psalm 27:4 (emphasis added) "One *thing* have I desired of the LORD, that will I **seek** after; that I may dwell in the house of the LORD all the days of my life, to behold the beauty of the LORD and to enquire in his temple." (David desired, hungered, thirsted and

sought after God, to dwell in His house all the days of his life. Why? To behold His beauty! And to enquire, to ask. We don't find all the answers all the time, but we get enough of them to make us want to keep traveling on!)

Psalm 27:5 (emphasis added) "For in the time of trouble he shall **hide** me in his pavilion:" (In Old Testament Bible times a pavilion was the tent of the Commander-in-chief on the battlefield. It was the absolute safest place to be on the battlefield because the Commander was going to be protected above all else! God is our Commander, and His tent is the safest place. We fondly remember the old gospel hymn, "For I'm *safe in God's pavilion*, happy in His love and grace, And I'm living on the Hallelujah side."

Psalm 27:5 (emphasis added) "…in the **secret of his tabernacle** shall he **hide** me;" This wonderful passage was literally fulfilled in my life as I began worshipping at "The Tabernacle." I had just lost my beloved soulmate, Marcella, to ovarian cancer, and the Lord seemed to melt my broken heart and let my incense of praise and worship rise, a sweet-smelling savor to Him. God began turning my ambushes of grief into rendezvous of praise! I felt He was literally "**hiding me**" in "**the secret of his tabernacle,**" with the word "Tabernacle" illuminated brilliantly! And the "secret" was, clearly, the Worship and the Word, as well as a Tabernacle full of loving, caring, compassionate saints!

I felt every song, every sermon was especially for me. The praise team, the choir, the awesome band, and the ministerial staff ushered me to the throne of grace where I bowed, beholding His beauty, as God poured His healing balm into me. These wonderful words, "In the secret of his **tabernacle** shall he hide me," leapt from the pages of the Bible straightway into my heart! I knew it was God turning my tears of grief into tears of praise and thanksgiving, giving me the garment of praise for the spirit of heaviness! I drove home on cloud nine, feeling so refreshed and comforted. I couldn't wait to get back to The Tabernacle next week.

Psalm 27:5 (emphasis added) "…he shall set me up upon a rock." (This is not talking about being seen and glorified by men but about being set up on a solid rock foundation.)

Psalm 27:6 "And now shall mine head be lifted up above mine enemies round about me:" (Lifted up in honor, not a hanging.) "therefore will I offer in his **tabernacle** sacrifices of joy; I will sing, yea, I will sing praises unto the LORD."

Psalm 27:7 "Hear, O LORD, *when* I cry with my voice: have mercy also upon me, and answer me."

Psalm 27:8 (emphasis added) *"When thou saidst,* **Seek** ye my face; my heart said unto thee, Thy face, LORD, will I **seek**." (When we are facing trials, tragedies, and broken hearts, we desperately need to seek the face of the Lord, to behold His beauty and enquire in His temple. Like Hezekiah when he found out he was going to die, when your back's against the wall, "turn and face the wall," and cry out to God, seeking His face. God answered Hezekiah and told Isaiah to tell him, "I have heard thy prayer, I have seen thy tears; behold, I will add unto thy days fifteen years." Then we need to take time to listen to what He says and respond obediently.)

Psalm 27:14 "Wait on the LORD: be of good courage, and he shall strengthen thine heart: wait, I say, on the LORD."

It is noteworthy that "**hide**" is used twice in Psalm 27, in verse 5, and "**seek**" is used three times, twice in verse 8 and again in verse 4.

It's Time to Find a Hiding Place

Exodus 33:21-22 (emphasis added) "And the LORD said, Behold, *there is a place by me*, and thou shalt stand upon a rock: And it shall come to pass, while my glory passeth by, that *I will put thee in a clift of the rock*, and *will cover thee with my hand* while I pass by:"

Psalm 27:5 (emphasis added) "For in the time of trouble he shall **hide me in his pavilion: in the secret of his tabernacle shall he hide me**; he shall set me up upon a rock."

Psalm 17:8 (emphasis added) "Keep me as the apple of the eye, **hide me under the shadow of thy wings**."

Psalm 31:20 (emphasis added) "Thou shalt **hide them in the secret of thy presence** from the pride of man: thou shalt **keep them secretly in a pavilion** from the strife of tongues."

Psalm 32:7 (emphasis added) "**Thou *art* my hiding place**; thou shalt preserve me from trouble; thou shalt compass me about with songs of deliverance. Selah."

Psalm 61:3 (emphasis added) "For thou hast been a **shelter** for me, and a **strong tower** from the enemy."

Isaiah 4:6 (emphasis added) "And there shall be a **tabernacle** for **a shadow in the daytime from the heat**, and for **a place of refuge**, and for **a covert** ["**hiding place,**" NIV] from storm and from rain."

Isaiah 49:2 (emphasis added) "And he hath made my mouth like a sharp sword; in the **shadow of his hand** hath **he hid me**, and made me a polished shaft; **in his quiver** hath **he hid me**."

It's Time to Seek the Lord

Hosea 10:12 (emphasis added) "Sow to yourselves in righteousness, reap in mercy; break up your fallow ground: for *it is* time to **seek** the LORD, till he come and rain righteousness upon you."

2 Chronicles 7:14 (emphasis added) "If my people, which are called by my name, shall humble themselves, and pray, and **seek** my face, and turn from their wicked ways; then will I hear from heaven, and will forgive their sin, and will heal their land."

Proverbs 8:17 (emphasis added) "I love them that love me; and those that **seek** me early shall find me."

Isaiah 55:6 (emphasis added) "**Seek** ye the LORD while he may be found, call ye upon him while he is near:" And the Bible clearly teaches He is near to the broken-hearted in Psalm 34:18, "The LORD *is* nigh unto them that are of a broken heart; and saveth such as be of a contrite spirit." So, since our broken hearts bring the Lord near, we should seek Him with all our hearts."

Jeremiah 29:13 (emphasis added) "And ye shall **seek** me, and find me, when ye shall search for me with all your heart."

Matthew 6:33 (emphasis added) "But **seek** ye first the kingdom of God, and his righteousness; and all these things shall be added unto you."

Luke 11:9 (emphasis added) "And I say unto you, Ask, and it shall be given you; **seek**, and ye shall find; knock, and it shall be opened unto you."

Hebrews 11:6 (emphasis added) "...he that cometh to God must believe that he is, and *that* he is a rewarder of them that diligently **seek** him."

It's Time to "Hide and Seek!"

SOLACE FROM THE PSALMS
FOR SENIORS

Psa 37:25 I have been young, and now am old; yet have I not seen the righteous forsaken, nor his seed begging bread.

Psa 71:9,12 Cast me not off in the time of old age; forsake me not when my strength faileth... O God, be not far from me: O my God, make haste for my help.

Psa 71:14 But I will hope continually, and will yet praise thee more and more.

Psa 71:18 Now also when I am old and grayheaded, O God, forsake me not; until I have shewed thy strength unto this generation, and thy power to every one that is to come.

Psa 90:12 So teach us to number our days, that we may apply our hearts unto wisdom.

Psa 90:17 And let the beauty of the LORD our God be upon us: and establish thou the work of our hands upon us; yea, the work of our hands establish thou it.

Psa 91:15,16 He shall call upon me, and I will answer him: I will be with him in trouble; I will deliver him, and honour him. With long life will I satisfy him, and shew him my salvation.

Psa 92:13,14 Those that be planted in the house of the LORD shall flourish in the courts of our God. They shall still bring forth fruit in old age; they shall be fat and flourishing;

Psa 103:2-5 Bless the LORD, O my soul, and forget not all his benefits: Who forgiveth all thine iniquities; who healeth all thy diseases; Who redeemeth thy life from destruction; who crowneth thee with lovingkindness and tender mercies; Who satisfieth thy mouth with good things; so that thy youth is renewed like the eagle's.

Bonus Scriptures:

Pro 3:1,2 My son, forget not my law; but let thine heart keep my commandments: For length of days, and long life, and peace, shall they add to thee.

Pro 9:11 For by me [wisdom] thy days shall be multiplied, and the years of thy life shall be increased.

Isa 46:4 And even to your old age I am he; and even to hoar hairs will I carry you: I have made, and I will bear; even I will carry, and will deliver you.

A PORTRAIT OF CALVARY
The Amazing 22nd Psalm

The Twenty-second Psalm seems like a dwarf when compared to its more popular neighbor, the Twenty-third Psalm. We can easily overlook Psalm twenty-two as we breeze past it seeking the comfort and strength from everyone's all-time favorite, the Shepherd Psalm.

What is so amazing about Psalm twenty-two? Simply this: although written one thousand years before Christ, it provides a detailed portrait of Calvary, portraying in graphic detail the express image of His suffering at Calvary — long before the Romans practiced crucifixion.

Fulfilled prophecy has always been one of the greatest proofs for the divine inspiration of the Word of God. Sprinkled throughout the Old Testament are many prophetic passages that were fulfilled in the New Testament. They often occur in single passages such as Genesis 3:15, Isaiah 7:14, Micah 5:2, and Zechariah 9:9. But, amazingly, the Twenty-second Psalm is jam-packed with more than twenty prophetic verses. This surely ranks it along with Isaiah fifty-three as one of the richest veins of fulfilled prophecy in the Bible — a veritable gold mine of divine inspiration.

Psalm 22:1 opens with the verbatim words Jesus cried in agony on the cross: "My God, my God, why hast thou forsaken me?" (See Matthew 27:46.) In verse 2, the words, "I cry in the ... night season," probably refer to the three-hour darkness at the height of His suffering. Verse 3 begins, "Thou art holy" reflecting why He felt forsaken, for He was made "to be sin for us" (2 Corinthians 5:21), and a holy God "canst not look on iniquity" (Habakkuk 1:13).

I Am a Worm?

A profound insight is hidden in verse 6: "But I am a worm, and no man." Surely this cannot be prophetic of Christ? But it is! The Hebrew word for "worm" is translated as "crimson" in Isaiah 1:18:

135

"though they [your sins] be red like crimson, they shall be as wool."
It refers to the crimson grub worm from which the ancient Israelites
obtained their red dyes. Henry Morris in *The Defender's Study Bible*
notes, "The female worm of this species, when laying her eggs,
affixes her body to a wood surface on which she will die after the
young are born."[54] The scarlet worm stains the wood, herself and
her young a crimson red! In like manner, the children of God are
redeemed by "the precious blood of Christ" (1 Peter 1:19). The
crimson worm paints a perfect picture of Jesus' sacrificial death
giving us eternal life!

The taunting of Christ on the cross is vividly portrayed in verses
7 and 8: "All they that see me laugh me to scorn: they shoot out
the lip, they shake the head, saying, He trusted on the Lord that he
would deliver him: let him deliver him, seeing he delighted in him."
(See Matthew 27:39,43.)

Verse 10 alludes to Christ's miraculous conception and birth: "I was
cast upon thee from the womb: thou art my God from my mother's
belly."

Verse 13 declares, "They gaped upon me with their mouths, as
a ravening and a roaring lion." Satan is referred to as "a roaring
lion" (1 Peter 5:8). Christ was also "compassed" by bulls, dogs, and
unicorns in verses 12, 16, and 21. This is a horrible picture of demon-
influenced men or wicked spirits gleefully taunting and celebrating
the death of Christ, unaware that the head of the serpent was here
receiving its lethal "bruise" (See Genesis 3:15). The tried Victim was
here becoming the triumphant Victor. "Having spoiled principalities
and powers, he made a show of them openly, triumphing over them
in it" at "his cross" (Colossians 2:14-15). "That through death he
might destroy him that had the power of death, that is, the devil"
(Hebrews 2:14).

Gambling for His Garments

The excruciating sufferings involved in the crucifixion are revealed
in verse 14: "I am poured out like water, and all my bones are out of
joint: my heart is like wax; it is melted in the midst of my bowels."

When the spear pierced His side, blood and water gushed out (See John 19:34). Evidently, the pull of gravity, coupled with His writhing in agony and muscular cramping, caused a separation of His bone joints and a collapse of His heart cavity.

The Lord's extreme thirst is pictured in verse 15: "My tongue cleaveth to my jaws."

Verse 16 declares, "For dogs have compassed me: the assembly of the wicked have enclosed me: they pierced my hands and my feet." The "dogs" could possibly refer to sodomites as the parallel construction of Deuteronomy 23:17-18 implies. (See also Revelation 22:15.) His pierced hands are clearly described in John 20:25-27.

Verse 18 foretells, "They part my garments among them, and cast lots upon my vesture." This bizarre action was one of the few events that God chose to highlight in all four gospels (Matthew 27:35; Mark 15:24; Luke 23:34; John 19:24). Matthew and John specifically state that it was done to fulfill this very verse of Scripture.

It's Time to Praise Him!

The focus of Psalm 22 abruptly changes from that of suffering to praise in verse 22: "In the midst of the congregation will I praise thee." He paid the price for our sins and now it is time to praise Him. It is noteworthy that this is the first mention of the verb "praise" (*hallal*) in the Psalms, which is Israel's book of praises. The theme of praise continues through verses 23-27: "Ye that fear the Lord, praise him ... glorify him ... My praise shall be of thee in the great congregation ... The meek shall eat and be satisfied: they shall praise the Lord that seek him ... and all the kindreds of the nations shall worship before thee." How very appropriate to praise our Lord and Savior on this awesome occasion of His triumphant victory over death and sin.

It Is Finished

Verses 30 and 31 provide a fitting conclusion to this psalm: "A seed shall serve him ... They shall come, and shall declare his righteousness unto a people that shall be born, that he hath done this." His seed, which is born again because of His sacrificial death, will "declare his righteousness" and His sacrificial death to "a people that shall be born," and they will be born again of water and the Spirit (John 3:5-7). They will declare that "he hath done this" — literally, "It is finished" (John 19:30).

Psalm 22 clearly shows that Calvary was not an afterthought — it was God's plan from the beginning: He was "... the Lamb slain from the foundation of the world" (Revelation 13:8). And best of all, He did it for us! Now, the next verse, "The Lord is my shepherd" (Psalm 23:1), means more to me than ever before. Praise God for the prophetic "Portrait of Calvary" in His amazing Twenty-second Psalm!

SOLACE FROM THE PSALMS

God's Rx for Fear & Anxiety
Take as Often as Needed, No Harmful Side Effects

Psa 1:1-3 Blessed is the man that walketh not in the counsel of the ungodly...But his delight is in the law of the LORD; and in his law doth he meditate day and night. And he shall be like a tree planted by the rivers of water… and whatsoever he doeth shall prosper.

Psa 3:2-3 Many there be which say of my soul, There is no help for him in God. Selah. But thou, O LORD, art a shield for me; my glory, and the lifter up of mine head.

Psa 4:7-8 Thou hast put gladness in my heart, more than in the time that their corn and their wine increased. I will both lay me down in peace, and sleep: for thou, LORD, only makest me dwell in safety.

Psa 5:11-12 But let all those that put their trust in thee rejoice: let them ever shout for joy, because thou defendest them: let them also that love thy name be joyful in thee. For thou, LORD, wilt bless the righteous; with favour wilt thou compass [surround] him as with a shield.

Psa 16:11 Thou wilt shew me the path of life: in thy presence is fulness of joy; at thy right hand there are pleasures for evermore.

Psa 17:8 Keep me as the apple of the eye, hide me under the shadow of thy wings...

Psa 18:2 The LORD is my rock, and my fortress, and my deliverer; my God, my strength, in whom I will trust; my buckler, and the horn of my salvation, and my high tower.

Psa 18:18-19 But the LORD was my stay. He brought me forth also into a large place; he delivered me, because he delighted in me.

Psa 18:32-33,36 It is God that girdeth me with strength, and maketh my way perfect. He maketh my feet like hinds' feet, and setteth me upon my high places. Thou hast enlarged my steps under me, that my feet did not slip.

Psa 22:3 But thou art holy, O thou that inhabitest the praises of Israel.

Psa 23:1-4 The LORD is my shepherd; I shall not want. He maketh me to lie down in green pastures: he leadeth me beside the still waters. He restoreth my soul: he leadeth me in the paths of righteousness for his name's sake. Yea, though I walk through the valley of the shadow of death, I will fear no evil: for thou art with me; thy rod and thy staff they comfort me.

Psa 23:5-6 Thou preparest a table before me in the presence of mine enemies: thou anointest my head with oil; my cup runneth over. Surely goodness and mercy shall follow me all the days of my life: and I will dwell in the house of the LORD for ever.

Psa 27:4 One thing have I desired of the LORD, that will I seek after; that I may dwell in the house of the LORD all the days of my life, to behold the beauty of the LORD, and to enquire in his temple.

Psa 27:5 For in the time of trouble he shall hide me in his pavilion: in the secret of his tabernacle shall he hide me; he shall set me up upon a rock.

Psa 27:10 When my father and my mother forsake me, then the LORD will take me up.

Psa 27:14 Wait on the LORD: be of good courage, and he shall strengthen thine heart: wait, I say, on the LORD.

Psa 28:7 The LORD is my strength and my shield; my heart trusted in him, and I am helped: therefore my heart greatly rejoiceth; and with my song will I praise him.

Psa 30:2-3 O LORD my God, I cried unto thee, and thou hast healed me. O LORD, thou hast brought up my soul from the grave: thou hast kept me alive, that I should not go down to the pit.

Psa 30:5 ...weeping may endure for a night, but joy cometh in the morning.

Psa 30:11 Thou hast turned for me my mourning into dancing: thou hast...girded me with gladness;

Psa 31:7-8 I will be glad and rejoice in thy mercy: for thou hast considered my trouble; thou hast known my soul in adversities; And hast not shut me up into the hand of the enemy: thou hast set my feet in a large room.

Psa 31:20-21 Thou shalt hide them in the secret of thy presence from the pride of man: thou shalt keep them secretly in a pavilion from the strife of tongues. Blessed be the LORD: for he hath shewed me his marvelous kindness in a strong city.

Psa 32:7 Thou art my hiding place; thou shalt preserve me from trouble; thou shalt compass me about with songs of deliverance. Selah.

Psa 34:7-8 The angel of the LORD encampeth round about them that fear him, and delivereth them. O taste and see that the LORD is good: blessed is the man that trusteth in him.

Psa 34:18-19 The LORD is nigh unto them that are of a broken heart; and saveth such as be of a contrite spirit. Many are the afflictions of the righteous: but the LORD delivereth him out of them all.

Psa 36:7-9 How excellent is thy lovingkindness, O God! therefore the children of men put their trust under the shadow of thy wings... and thou shalt make them drink of the river of thy pleasures. For with thee is the fountain of life...

Psa 37:3-4 Trust in the LORD, and do good; so shalt thou dwell in the land, and verily thou shalt be fed. Delight thyself also in the LORD; and he shall give thee the desires of thine heart.

Psa 40:2-3 He brought me up also out of an horrible pit, out of the miry clay, and set my feet upon a rock, and established my goings. And he hath put a new song in my mouth, even praise unto our God...

Psa 40:16-17 Let all those that seek thee rejoice and be glad in thee: let such as love thy salvation say continually, The LORD be magnified...thou art my help and my deliverer;

Psa 42:8 Yet the LORD will command his lovingkindness in the daytime, and in the night his song shall be with me, and my prayer unto the God of my life.

Psa 42:11 Why art thou cast down, O my soul? and why art thou disquieted within me? hope thou in God: for I shall yet praise him, who is the health of my countenance, and my God. (Also 42:5 and 43:5!).

Psa 43:3-4 O send out thy light and thy truth: let them lead me; let them bring me unto thy holy hill, and to thy tabernacles. Then will I go unto the altar of God, unto God my exceeding joy:

Psa 46:1 God is our refuge and strength, a very [intensively] present help in trouble.

Psa 46:10 Be still, and know that I am God: I will be exalted among the heathen, I will be exalted in the earth.

Psa 48:14 For this God is our God for ever and ever: he will be our guide even unto death.

Psa 49:15 But God will redeem my soul from the power of the grave: for he shall receive me. Selah.

Psa 50:15 And call upon me in the day of trouble: I will deliver thee, and thou shalt glorify me.

Psa 51:17 The sacrifices of God are a broken spirit: a broken and a contrite heart, O God, thou wilt not despise.

Psa 55:17-18 Evening, and morning, and at noon, will I pray, and cry aloud: and he shall hear my voice. He hath delivered my soul in peace from the battle that was against me:

Psa 55:22 Cast thy burden upon the LORD, and he shall sustain thee: he shall never suffer the righteous to be moved.

Psa 56:3-4 What time I am afraid, I will trust in thee. In God I will praise his word, in God I have put my trust; I will not fear what flesh can do unto me.

Psa 56:8,12-13 Put thou my tears into thy bottle: are they not in thy book? Thy vows are upon me, O God: I will render praises unto thee. For thou hast delivered my soul from death: wilt not thou deliver my feet from falling, that I may walk before God in the light of the living? (Also Psa 116:8,9).

Psa 57:1-3 Be merciful unto me, O God, be merciful unto me: for my soul trusteth in thee: yea, in the shadow of thy wings will I make my refuge, until these calamities be overpast. I will cry unto God most high; unto God that performeth all things for me. He shall send from heaven, and save me from the reproach of him that would swallow me up. (Also 63:7)

Psa 60:12 Through God we shall do valiantly: for he it is that shall tread down our enemies.

Psa 61:1-3 Hear my cry, O God; attend unto my prayer. From the end of the earth will I cry unto thee, when my heart is overwhelmed: lead me to the rock that is higher than I. For thou hast been a shelter for me, and a strong tower from the enemy.

Psa 63:3 Because thy lovingkindness is better than life, my lips shall praise thee.

Psa 63:7-8 Because thou hast been my help, therefore in the shadow of thy wings will I rejoice. My soul followeth hard after thee: thy right hand upholdeth me.

Psa 64:10 The righteous shall be glad in the LORD, and shall trust in him; and all the upright in heart shall glory.

Psa 66:12 We went through fire and through water: but thou broughtest us out into a wealthy place.

Psa 66:19-20 But verily God hath heard me; he hath attended to the voice of my prayer. Blessed be God, which hath not turned away my prayer, nor his mercy from me.

Psa 67:1 God be merciful unto us, and bless us; and cause his face to shine upon us; Selah.

Psa 68:6 God setteth the solitary in families: he bringeth out those which are bound with chains:

Psa 68:19-20 Blessed be the Lord, who daily loadeth us with benefits, even the God of our salvation. Selah. He that is our God is the God of salvation; and unto GOD the Lord belong the issues [NIV: escape] from death.

Psa 70:4 Let all those that seek thee rejoice and be glad in thee: and let such as love thy salvation say continually, Let God be magnified.

Psa 71:9 Cast me not off in the time of old age; forsake me not when my strength faileth.

Psa 71:14 But I will hope continually, and will yet praise thee more and more.

Psa 71:16 I will go in the strength of the Lord GOD: I will make mention of thy righteousness, even of thine only.

Psa 71:18 Now also when I am old and grayheaded, O God, forsake me not; until I have shewed thy strength unto this generation, and thy power to every one that is to come.

Psa 71:20-21 Thou, which hast shewed me great and sore troubles, shalt quicken me again, and shalt bring me up again from the depths of the earth ... and comfort me on every side.

Psa 72:12 For he shall deliver the needy when he crieth; the poor also, and him that hath no helper.

Psa 73:23 Nevertheless I am continually with thee: thou hast holden me by my right hand.

Psa 73:26 My flesh and my heart faileth: but God is the strength of my heart, and my portion for ever.

Psa 73:28 But it is good for me to draw near to God: I have put my trust in the Lord GOD...

Psa 77:10 And I said, This is my infirmity: but I will remember the years of the right hand of the most High.

Psa 78:72 So he fed them according to the integrity of his heart; and guided them by the skilfulness of his hands.

Psa 84:10-11 For a day in thy courts is better than a thousand... For the LORD God is a sun and shield: the LORD will give grace and glory: no good thing will he withhold from them that walk uprightly.

Psa 86:17 Shew me a token for good;... because thou, LORD, hast holpen [helped] me, and comforted me.

Psa 89:15-16 Blessed is the people that know the joyful sound: they shall walk, O LORD, in the light of thy countenance. In thy name shall they rejoice all the day: and in thy righteousness shall they be exalted.

Psa 90:15 Make us glad according to the days wherein thou hast afflicted us [NIV: for as many days as you have afflicted us], and the years wherein we have seen evil [NIV: for as many years as we have seen trouble.]

Psa 90:17 And let the beauty of the LORD our God be upon us:

Psa 91:1-2 He that dwelleth in the secret place of the most High shall abide under the shadow of the Almighty. I will say of the LORD, He is my refuge and my fortress: my God; in him will I trust.

Psa 91:11 For he shall give his angels charge over thee, to keep thee in all thy ways.

Psa 91:15, 16 He shall call upon me, and I will answer him: I will be with him in trouble; I will deliver him, and honour him. With long life will I satisfy him, and shew him my salvation.

Psa 92:1 It is a good thing to give thanks unto the LORD, and to sing praises unto thy name, O most High:

Psa 92:13-14 Those that be planted in the house of the LORD shall flourish in the courts of our God. They shall still bring forth fruit in old age; they shall be fat and flourishing;

Psa 94:18-19 When I said, My foot slippeth; thy mercy, O LORD, held me up. In the multitude of my thoughts within me thy comforts delight my soul.

Psa 96:9 O worship the LORD in the beauty of holiness: fear before him, all the earth.

Psa 97:10 Ye that love the LORD, hate evil: he preserveth the souls of his saints; he delivereth them out of the hand of the wicked.

Psa 98:4 Make a joyful noise unto the LORD, all the earth: make a loud noise, and rejoice, and sing praise.

Psa 100:1-5 Make a joyful noise unto the LORD, all ye lands. Serve the LORD with gladness: come before his presence with singing. Know ye that the LORD he is God: it is he that hath made us, and not we ourselves; we are his people, and the sheep of his pasture. Enter into his gates with thanksgiving, and into his courts with praise: be thankful unto him, and bless his name. For the LORD is good; his mercy is everlasting; and his truth endureth to all generations.

Psa 102:1-2 Hear my prayer, O LORD, and let my cry come unto thee. Hide not thy face from me in the day when I am in trouble; incline thine ear unto me: in the day when I call answer me speedily.

Psa 103:2-5 Bless the LORD, O my soul, and forget not all his benefits: Who forgiveth all thine iniquities; who healeth all thy diseases; Who redeemeth thy life from destruction; who crowneth thee with lovingkindness and tender mercies; Who satisfieth thy mouth with good things; so that thy youth is renewed like the eagle's.

Psa 104:33-34 I will sing unto the LORD as long as I live: I will sing praise to my God while I have my being. My meditation of him shall be sweet: I will be glad in the LORD.

Psa 105:3,4 Glory ye in his holy name: let the heart of them rejoice that seek the LORD. Seek the LORD, and his strength: seek his face evermore.

Psa 107:13-14 Then they cried unto the LORD in their trouble, and he saved them out of their distresses. He brought them out of darkness and the shadow of death, and brake their bands in sunder.

Psa 107:20 He sent his word, and healed them, and delivered them from their destructions (NIV: rescued them from the grave.)

Psa 107:28-30 Then they cry unto the LORD in their trouble, and he bringeth them out of their distresses. He maketh the storm a calm, so that the waves thereof are still. Then are they glad because they be quiet; so he bringeth them unto their desired haven.

Psa 108:12-13 Give us help from trouble: for vain is the help of man.Through God we shall do valiantly: for he it is that shall tread down our enemies.

Psa 116:12-13 What shall I render unto the LORD for all his benefits toward me? I will take the cup of salvation, and call upon the name of the LORD.

Psa 118:5-6 I called upon the LORD in distress: the LORD answered me, and set me in a large place. The LORD is on my side; I will not fear: what can man do unto me?

Psa 118:14,17-18 The LORD is my strength and song, and is become my salvation. I shall not die, but live, and declare the works of the LORD. The LORD hath chastened me sore: but he hath not given me over unto death.

Psa 118:24 This is the day which the LORD hath made; we will rejoice and be glad in it.

Psa 119:49-50 Remember the word unto thy servant, upon which thou hast caused me to hope. This is my comfort in my affliction: for thy word hath quickened me.

Psa 119:71 It is good for me that I have been afflicted; that I might learn thy statutes.

Psa 119:75-77 I know, O LORD, that thy judgments are right, and that thou in faithfulness hast afflicted me. Let, I pray thee, thy merciful kindness be for my comfort, according to thy word unto thy servant. Let thy tender mercies come unto me, that I may live: for thy law is my delight.

Psa 119:89-90 For ever, O LORD, thy word is settled in heaven. Thy faithfulness is unto all generations: thou hast established the earth, and it abideth.

Psa 119:105 Thy word is a lamp unto my feet, and a light unto my path.

Psa 119:114 Thou art my hiding place and my shield: I hope in thy word.

Psa 119:116-117 Uphold me according unto thy word, that I may live: and let me not be ashamed of my hope. Hold thou me up, and I shall be safe: and I will have respect unto thy statutes continually.

Psa 119:133 Order my steps in thy word: and let not any iniquity have dominion over me.

Psa 121:2,5 My help cometh from the LORD, which made heaven and earth. The LORD is thy keeper: the LORD is thy shade upon thy right hand.

Psa 121:7-8 The LORD shall preserve thee from all evil: he shall preserve thy soul. The LORD shall preserve thy going out and thy coming in from this time forth, and even for evermore.

Psa 124:7-8 Our soul is escaped as a bird out of the snare of the fowlers: the snare is broken, and we are escaped. Our help is in the name of the LORD, who made heaven and earth.

Psa 126:5-6 They that sow in tears shall reap in joy. He that goeth forth and weepeth, bearing precious seed, shall doubtless come again with rejoicing, bringing his sheaves with him.

Psa 128:2-3 For thou shalt eat the labour of thine hands: happy shalt thou be, and it shall be well with thee. Thy wife shall be as a fruitful vine by the sides of thine house: thy children like olive plants round about thy table.

Psa 130:5 I wait for the LORD, my soul doth wait, and in his word do I hope.

Psa 138:3 In the day when I cried thou answeredst me, and strengthenedst me with strength in my soul.

Psa 139:5-6 Thou hast beset me behind and before, and laid thine hand upon me. Such knowledge is too wonderful for me; it is high, I cannot attain unto it.

Psa 142:5,7 I cried unto thee, O LORD: I said, Thou art my refuge and my portion in the land of the living. Bring my soul out of prison, that I may praise thy name: the righteous shall compass me about; for thou shalt deal bountifully with me.

Psa 144:15 Happy is that people, that is in such a case: yea, happy is that people, whose God is the LORD.

Psa 145:1-3 I will extol thee, my God, O king; and I will bless thy name for ever and ever. Every day will I bless thee; and I will praise thy name for ever and ever. Great is the LORD, and greatly to be praised; and his greatness is unsearchable.

Psa 145:8-9 The LORD is gracious, and full of compassion; slow to anger, and of great mercy. The LORD is good to all: and his tender mercies are over all his works.

Psa 145:14,18 The LORD upholdeth all that fall, and raiseth up all those that be bowed down. The LORD is nigh unto all them that call upon him, to all that call upon him in truth.

Psa 145:20-21 The LORD preserveth all them that love him: but all the wicked will he destroy. My mouth shall speak the praise of the LORD: and let all flesh bless his holy name for ever and ever.

Psa 146:2 While I live will I praise the LORD: I will sing praises unto my God while I have any being.

Psa 147:3 He healeth the broken in heart, and bindeth up their wounds.

Psa 150:6 Let every thing that hath breath praise the LORD. Praise ye the LORD.

Ron Schoolcraft

Ecclesiastes and Psalms for "Seasoned Saints"
(Also, for "All Ages")

We "Seasoned Saints" heartily invite the younger generations to join us as we take a romp through Ecclesiastes 12 and various encouraging Psalms for some wonderful wisdom from the Word God gave us. You may find yourself laughing (with us) or praying (for us) as you get a preview of what lies ahead (for you!) This is God's inspired Word, so it is very "profitable" (for all of us): "All scripture is given by inspiration of God [Greek, *theopneustos*, meaning 'God-breathed'], and is *profitable* for doctrine, for reproof, for correction, for instruction in righteousness" (2 Timothy 3:16, emphasis added

First, a note about the meaning of the word, "Ecclesiastes." It's a Jewish Greek Septuagint word equivalent to the Hebrew word translated "The Preacher." Hence, we get "ecclesiastical," meaning, concerning the clergy, or ministers. Both Jews and Christians believe Solomon wrote this book. Most scholars believe he probably wrote it in his old age, while looking back on happy, earlier years, and regretting his tragic failures in later years when his many wives and concubines turned his heart from the Lord. (See 1 Kings 11:1-4, 9).

There is an element of sadness in Ecclesiastes, and one can get weary of reading: "vanity of vanities, all is vanity (meaningless) and vexation of the spirit; this also is vanity and vexation of spirit; there is nothing better than to eat, drink and be merry; sorrow is better than laughter; and the heart of the wise is in the house of mourning." But still there are numerous wise sayings, as in the book of Proverbs, powerful theological truths, and striking spiritual insights. A deeper purpose seems to be to convince young people of the vanity and futility of worldly learning, riches, and pleasures, while exhorting them to remember their Creator in the days of their youth.

Remember Now Thy Creator

Ecclesiastes 12:1 "Remember now thy Creator in the days of thy youth ..." This has always been one of our favorite Scriptures. And it *still* is even today! Since we Seasoned Saints *still remember* our Creator, it follows, we must *still be* "in the days of our youth!" We confess to being "*young* at heart," and entering our "second *childhood*," but this verse still offers us some hope! We like the age guidelines that someone has suggested: when we enter our sixties and seventies, we reach the *youth* of old age; when we enter our eighties and nineties, we arrive at the *middle-age* of old age.

Ecclesiastes 12:1 continues, telling us *why* we should remember our Creator in the days of our youth: "...while the evil days come not, nor the years draw nigh, when thou shalt say, I have no pleasure in them." How many can remember reading this verse as a youth, not at all concerned about aging, and thinking, *it will never happen to me*? Oops! In the next few verses, the Preacher makes use of metaphors to reveal a picturesque description of old age:

Signs of "Seasoning"

Ecclesiastes 12:3 "In the day when the keepers of the house shall tremble, and the strong men shall bow themselves, and the grinders cease because they are few, and those that look out of the windows be darkened." The "house" is the aging body, and the "keepers of the house" are the hands and arms that tremble; the "strong men" are the legs and backbone which bow themselves; the "grinders" are the teeth, which cease because they are few; and the "windows" are the eyes, dimmed by cataracts.

Ecclesiastes 12:4 "And the doors shall be shut in the streets, when the sound of the grinding is low, and he shall rise up at the voice of the bird, and all the daughters of musick shall be brought low." The closed "doors" are difficulty in speaking; the "low sound" represents the difficulty of hearing; "rise up at the voice of the bird" speaks of the difficulty of sleeping; and "all the daughters of music ... brought low" is the deterioration of the vocal chords and singing.

Ecclesiastes 12:5 "Also when they shall be afraid of that which is high, and fears shall be in the way, and the almond tree shall flourish, and the grasshopper shall be a burden, and desire shall fail: because man goeth to his long home, and the mourners go about the streets." The fear of heights suggests the fear of the danger of falling while walking; fear of being "in the way" implies concerns about the inability to protect oneself; the "almond tree," white hair, shall flourish; the "grasshopper shall be a burden," means irritation by the continuous buzzing of locusts; "desire" for pleasure fades and "fails" and the "long home" and "mourners" reveal that death finally comes. This is clearly shown in the next two verses also.

Ecclesiastes 12:6 "Or ever the silver cord be loosed, or the golden bowl be broken, or the pitcher be broken at the fountain, or the wheel broken at the cistern."

Ecclesiastes 12:7 "Then shall the dust return to the earth as it was: and the spirit shall return unto God who gave it." After all the sadness, some good news: "The spirit shall return to God who gave it." Jesus confirmed this when He told the thief on the cross, "To day shalt thou be with me in paradise" (Luke 23:43). The apostle Paul made this clear to the Corinthian church: "We are confident, I say, and willing rather to be absent from the body, and to be present with the Lord" (2 Corinthians 5:8).

Forgetfulness, Anyone?

Perhaps Solomon's age caught up with him: it seems he "forgot" to mention "FORGETFULNESS," as one of the Seasoned Saints' crowning *virtues*. (Well, maybe that's why he had to admonish all to "REMEMBER now thy Creator ...."). Oh, the stories Seasoned Saints could tell about forgetfulness. One of the most common and most hilarious (until it happens to you) is: going into a room then completely forgetting why! We just stand there embarrassed, wracking our brains and memories, wondering why we entered. The author humbly advances this explanation: the brains of

Seasoned Saints are jam-packed with tons of volatile information (maybe several gigabytes worth)! We have accumulated much more knowledge than when we were younger. So, while entering the room, three or four other urgent tasks pop into our minds, crowding out the original one. This is why you will see notepads and lists of things to do, scattered randomly through our homes. But, while looking for a notepad to write it down, three or four other tasks ... We do need the wisdom of ... oh, what's his name?!

Time would fail us in trying to entertain you with our many hilarious stories about forgetting names, and misplacing our glasses, cell phones, car keys, etc. ("You're wearing them!" "What's that in your hand?") LOL. SMH. Oh yes, we incorporate abbreviations in our texts. But I caution all to be careful to find out the meaning before using them. Some are obscene. But there is one that has stumped me. Nobody seems to know what IDK means. Everyone tells me they don't know. LOL. SMH. Please, if you don't know what IDK means, don't bother telling me that you don't know. I already know that.... LOL.

Solomon's Conclusion

Ecclesiastes 12:13 "Let us hear the conclusion of the whole matter: Fear God, and keep his commandments: for this *is* the whole *duty* of man." Here is the conclusion of the wisest man who ever lived (except for Jesus Christ). What is the whole duty of man? It is *not* to get all the riches, fame, and women he can accumulate, but to *fear God and keep his commandments*. The next verse explains why.

Ecclesiastes 12:14 "For God shall bring every work into judgment, with every secret thing, whether it be good, or whether it be evil." Judgement day is coming!

If Solomon could have written Ecclesiastes in New Testament times, He might have written: "Remember now thy Creator, *who became thy Savior*, in the days of thy youth." Remember now thy Creator who became one of us and robed Himself in flesh so He could suffer an excruciatingly painful death of maximum pain for maximum time, and "bare our sins in His own body on the tree," (1

Peter 2:24); and He was "made to be sin for us" (2 Corinthians 5:21). He was made to be a sinner, to redeem us. But Solomon, in all his wisdom, did not have a clue of what the Creator had planned. The Creator was going to turn the tables on Satan, who tried to wreck His Creation in the Garden of Eden. God was going to become one of us to die for us as a Victim at Calvary, then rise from the dead as the Victor, triumphing over Satan and taking back the keys of death and hell. In the original creation God's children could walk with him in the cool of the day. But now, after the Creator became our Savior, His children will be caught up to Heaven to see Him face to face. And they will attend a marriage supper, not as guests, but as the Bride of Christ, and be married to the Lamb! He became one of us so we could be one with Him. (See Revelation 19:7-9; 1 Timothy 3:16; and Ephesians 5:31-32).

"Thy Creator" Will *Remember You*!

Now, let's look at some **Psalms** that show us that if we will remember the Creator in our youth, He will remember us in our old age. We will reap what we sow.

Psalm 71 (A Prayer for the Aged)

Psalm 71:9 "Cast me not off in the time of old age; forsake me not when my strength faileth."

Psalm 71:12 "O God, be not far from me: O my God, make haste for my help."

Psalm 71:14 "But I will hope continually, and will yet praise thee more and more."

Psalm 71:17 "O God, thou hast taught me from my youth: and hitherto have I declared thy wondrous   works."

Psalm 71:18 "Now also when I am old and gray-headed, O God, forsake me not; until I have shewed thy strength unto *this* generation, *and* thy power to every one *that* is to come."

Psalm 90 (A Prayer of Moses the man of God.)

Psalm 90:10 "The days of our years *are* threescore years and ten; and if by reason of strength *they be* fourscore years, yet *is* their strength labour and sorrow; for it is soon cut off, and we fly away." (It is amazing that over three thousand years after Moses, with all the great strides in medical science that have been made, the normal life span is still only about seventy to eighty years!)

Psalm 90:12 "So teach us to number our days, that we may apply our hearts unto wisdom." "Redeeming the time, because the days are evil" (Ephesians 5:16). "And that, knowing the time, that now *it is* high time to awake out of sleep: for now *is* our salvation nearer than when we believed" (Romans 13:11).

Psalm 90:15 "Make us glad according to the days *wherein* thou hast afflicted us, *and* the years *wherein* we have seen evil." The CSB rendering is: "Make us rejoice for as many days as you have humbled us, for as many years as we have seen adversity." This great truth is confirmed in 2 Corinthians 4:17 "For our light affliction, which is but for a moment, worketh for us a far more exceeding *and* eternal weight of glory;" (Our light affliction is working *for* us? But I thought afflictions and trials worked *against* us? No, they work "*for us* a far more exceeding and eternal weight of glory." That "far more exceeding and eternal weight of glory" is, indeed, a "heavy weight". But the light affliction is a "light weight!" In summary: *lightweight trials bring heavyweight blessings*! The trials we go through cannot compare with the glory and blessings of Heaven and eternity with Jesus. What we are going through right now will bring heavyweight blessings soon!)

Psalm 90:17 "And let the beauty of the LORD our God be upon us: and establish thou the work of our hands upon us; yea, the work of our hands establish thou it."

Psalm 91 (Abiding Under the Shadow of the Almighty)

Psalm 91:1 "He that dwelleth in the secret place of the most High shall abide under the shadow of the Almighty."

Psalm 91:15 "He shall call upon me, and I will answer him: I *will be* with him in trouble; I will deliver him, and honour him."

Psalm 91:16 "With long life will I satisfy him, and shew him my salvation."

Psalm 92:13 "Those that be planted in the house of the LORD shall flourish in the courts of our God."

Psalm 92:14 "They shall still bring forth fruit in old age; they shall be fat and flourishing."

Psalm 103:5 "Who satisfieth thy mouth with good things; so that thy youth is renewed like the eagle's."

Bonus Blessings

Proverbs 3:1 "My son, forget not my law; but let thine heart keep my commandments:"

Proverbs 3:2 "For length of days, and long life, and peace, shall they add to thee."

Isaiah 46:4 "And *even* to *your* old age I *am* he; and *even* to hoar hairs will I carry *you:* I have made, and I will bear; even I will carry, and will deliver *you.* "

"Remember Now Thy Creator" and He will carry you, bear you up and deliver you when you reach old age! What an exceeding and eternal weight of glory and blessings! It's great to be numbered among the "Seasoned Saints!"

PART IV

THE GOOD NEWS

Remember the Resurrection

Jesus Christ commanded His apostles to remember His death: "This do in remembrance of me... For as often as ye eat this bread, and drink this cup, ye do shew the Lord's death till he come (1 Corinthians 11:24-26). And the apostle Paul instructed Timothy (and us), to remember His Resurrection: "Remember that Jesus Christ ... was raised from the dead..." (2 Timothy 2:8).

The Bible clearly identifies the Resurrection of Jesus Christ as crucial to the Christian message, as essential as the atoning death of Christ: "If Christ be not raised, your faith is vain; ye are yet in your sins" (1 Corinthians 15:17). Though His death atoned for our sins, without His resurrection our faith would be futile, and we would be yet in our sins.

But, praise God, He is risen! "But now is Christ risen from the dead, and become the firstfruits of them that slept" (1 Corinthians 15:20). Eugene Peterson, in his contemporary language version, *The Message*, rendered this verse: "But the truth is that Christ has been raised up, the first in a long legacy of those who are going to leave the cemeteries."

Many Infallible Proofs

In the Book of Acts the preaching of the apostles focused on the Resurrection: "With great power gave the apostles witness of the resurrection of the Lord Jesus" (Acts 4:33). Luke, the author, opened the Book of Acts with a reference to the Resurrection: "To whom also he shewed himself alive after His passion by many infallible proofs, being seen of them forty days" (Acts 1:3).

Dr. Henry Morris, in his *Defender's Study Bible*, has written, "The term 'infallible proofs' is one word in the Greek (*tekmerion*) and occurs only this one time. It means literally 'many criteria of certainty.' It is significant that the inspired Word of God applies it only to the resurrection of Christ." Morris has further noted that this term "emphasizes that the evidences for Christ's resurrection were not philosophical speculations but certain facts. No other event of biblical history has been confirmed more certainly than His bodily resurrection."[55]

What are some of these "infallible proofs"? In addition to the many infallible Scriptures, only a few of which are quoted herein, some of the proofs follow:

The Sealed Tomb.

At the instigation of the chief priests and Pharisees the tomb was sealed with a large stone and guarded by Roman soldiers, an act no doubt inspired by Satan in a feeble attempt to prevent the Resurrection. It served, rather, to substantiate it. It documented the miracle! For it is certain that the timid, fearful disciples would not have ventured out of hiding and overcome these obstacles to steal the body and perpetrate a fraud. "Let God arise, let his enemies be scattered: let them also that hate him flee before him" (Psalm 68:1). What happened to the Roman soldiers guarding the tomb? These enemies undoubtedly scattered and fled before Him!

The Empty Tomb.

The empty tomb has never been explained, except by the bodily resurrection. If the body were still there or any other place accessible to Jews or Romans, they would certainly have produced it as a sure means of immediately quenching the spreading flame of Christianity.

Eyewitnesses.

"For I delivered unto you first of all that which I also received, how that Christ died for our sins ... and that he was buried, and that he rose again the third day according to the scriptures: and that he was seen of Cephas, then of the twelve: after that, he was seen of above five hundred brethren at once; of whom the greater part remain unto this present" (1 Corinthians 15:3-6). This remarkable parade of eyewitnesses of the resurrected Christ is part of the overwhelming body of evidence making this a most certain fact of biblical history. In any court trial eyewitnesses are most important in persuading a jury.

The Change in the Disciples.

The apostles and disciples became bold almost overnight. From a little band of depressed, discouraged, despondent, and devastated disciples hiding in an upper room, they transformed into a company of firebrands that no amount of persecution could silence. The only reasonable explanation for this miraculous transformation is the certainty of their knowledge of the Resurrection coupled with their "endue[ment] with power from on high" (Luke 24:49) on the Day of Pentecost (Acts 2:1-4). They were fulfilling the promise of Acts 1:8: "But ye shall receive power, after that the Holy Ghost is come upon you: and ye shall be witnesses unto me both in Jerusalem and in all Judaea..." Witness the apostle Peter, who had cowardly denied the Lord three times, preaching a powerful message at Pentecost, boldly proclaiming the resurrection and demanding repentance of "every one of you" (Acts 2:14-40). Moreover, "When [the scribes, elders and high priest] saw the boldness of Peter and John, and perceived that they were unlearned and ignorant men, they marvelled; and they took knowledge of them, that they had been with Jesus" (Acts 4:13). The imagery here was that Peter and John had recently been in the presence of a living Jesus, not a dead one.

The Disciples' Willingness to Die.

No man would willingly sacrifice his life for something he knew to be a lie. Only the certain knowledge of the truth of Christ's resurrection could have caused the disciples to fearlessly face death. This fact substantiates the veracity of their message beyond all doubt. Of the twelve apostles listed in Acts 1:13, 26, only John died a natural death; history tells us the rest were martyred. The depressed, discouraged, despondent, and devastated disciples would not have suffered and died for a dead Messiah.

The Believers' Personal Experience.

A man with an experience is never at the mercy of a skeptic with an argument. We have been "enlightened, and have tasted of the heavenly gift and were made partakers of the Holy Ghost, and have tasted the good word of God, and the powers of the world to come" (Hebrews 6:4-5). Just as surely as Jesus was raised from the dead, we are also raised: "We are buried with him by baptism into death: that like as Christ was raised up from the dead by the glory of the Father, even so we also should walk in newness of life. For if we have been planted together in the likeness of his death, we shall also be in the likeness of his resurrection" (Romans 6:4-5). The awesome change Jesus Christ has made in our lives proves conclusively to us the truth of His resurrection. "If any man be in Christ, he is a new creature: old things are passed away; behold, all things are become new" (2 Corinthians 5:17).

Such "infallible proofs" as these prove that Jesus Christ has, indeed, conquered death itself, thereby demonstrating that He is the Creator of life and the only possible Savior to redeem us from sin and death! No wonder Peter could say, "For we have not followed cunningly devised fables, when we made known unto you the power and coming of our Lord Jesus Christ, but were eyewitnesses of his majesty" (2 Peter 1:16).

The Pharisees "Remembered" the Resurrection.

Jesus repeatedly forewarned the disciples that He would be killed and then resurrected. "The Son of man is delivered into the hands of men, and they shall kill him; and after that he is killed, he shall rise the third day" (Mark 9:31). (See also Matthew 16:21; 17:23; 20:19; Mark 8:31 and 10:34.) While the disciples languished in their grief, an amazing event was occurring at Pilate's palace: "The chief priests and Pharisees came together unto Pilate, saying, Sir, we *remember* that that deceiver said, while he was yet alive, After three days I will rise again. Command therefore that the sepulchre be made sure until the third day, lest his disciples come by night, and steal him away ..." (Matthew 27:62-64, emphasis added). How remarkably ironic that the enemies of Christ remembered the promise of His resurrection while His disciples cowered behind locked doors, the resurrection promise long forgotten. Nor did they remember it until after His resurrection (see John 2:22). Had the disciples remembered Jesus' words, it would have spared them much heart-rending grief. The more we remember His Words, the less grief we will bear.

The "Resurrection" at Pentecost.

On the Day of Pentecost Peter used a passage from a Psalm of David (Psalm 16:10), to preach the Resurrection: "Because thou wilt not leave my soul in hell, neither wilt thou suffer thine Holy One to see corruption" (Acts 2:27). Peter then declared that David did not fulfill this verse, for: "The patriarch David ... is both dead and buried, and his sepulchre is with us unto this day" (Acts 2:29). Peter then revealed whom David was prophesying about: "He seeing this before spake of the *resurrection of Christ*, that his soul was not left in hell, neither his flesh did see corruption. This Jesus hath God raised up, whereof we all are witnesses" (Acts 2:31-32).

A few verses later, at the conclusion of his message, Peter declared, "Repent, and be baptized every one of you in the name of Jesus Christ for the remission of sins, and ye shall receive the gift of the Holy Ghost. For the promise is unto you, and to your children, and to all that are afar off, even as many as the Lord our God shall call" (Acts 2:38-39). Peter's inspired ("God-breathed") conclusion is still imperative today, whenever and wherever the resurrection of Christ is preached.

It is noteworthy that, prior to the resurrection and Pentecost, Peter and the other disciples could not even remember or understand Jesus' straightforward promises of His coming death and resurrection, let alone the Messianic Old Testament prophecies. But after their Holy Ghost baptism they were transformed into powerful preachers of the Scriptures, especially of the Messianic prophecies.

The ultimate reason to keep the triumphant resurrection of Jesus Christ indelibly etched in our memory? It portends our own resurrection! "But if the Spirit of him that raised up Jesus from the dead dwell in you, he that raised up Christ from the dead shall also quicken your mortal bodies by his Spirit that dwelleth in you" (Romans 8:11).

A final Word from the Author and Finisher of our faith:

"I am he that liveth, and was dead; and, behold, I am alive forevermore, Amen; and have the keys of hell and of death" (Revelation 1:18).

GOD GAVE THE WORD

A HOME BIBLE STUDY
The Certainty of the Gospel

> That I might make thee know the certainty of the
> words of truth; that thou mightest answer the words
> of truth to them that send unto thee.
>
> Proverbs 22:21

We must first know the certainty of the Words of truth ourselves, before we can effectively "give an answer to every man that asketh …" (I Peter 3:15). This Home Bible Study will show the certainty of the Gospel of Jesus Christ in three parts:

1. The Gospel Beginning

2. The Gospel Commissioned

3. The Gospel Preached

Following each Scripture reference, an abbreviated summary of the passage is presented, followed by the author's comments in parentheses. The student is encouraged to turn in the Bible to each of these passages and study the context with an open mind as well as an open Bible.

1. The Gospel Beginning

Luke 1:1-4 "Forasmuch as many have taken in hand to set forth in order a declaration of those things which are most surely believed among us … It seemed good to me also, having had perfect understanding of all things from the very first, to write unto thee … That thou mightest know the certainty of those things …" (Luke declared that he, having had perfect understanding of the things most surely believed, would write that we might know their certainty. Luke also wrote the Book of Acts, so we will hear more from him in Part 2 and Part 3.)

Mark 1:1-8 "The beginning of the gospel of Jesus Christ. John did baptize and preach the baptism of repentance for the remission of sins ... And preached, saying ... I indeed have baptized with water but He shall baptize you with the Holy Ghost." (Here is a marvelous thing — God revealed to John the Baptist something about the Gospel: that repentance and water baptism would be essential and that Jesus would baptize with the Holy Ghost! See also parallel passages in Matthew 3:11 and Luke 3:16.)

John 3:1-7, 16, 21 "Except a man be born of water and the Spirit he cannot enter the kingdom of God ... Whosoever believeth in Him should not perish ... He that doeth truth cometh to the light." (Many isolate John 3:16, saying all you have to do is believe, but believing must include a birth of water and spirit or we have a contradiction. Is believing alone sufficient? James 2:19 says the devils believe and tremble. Are they saved? In this next passage, four chapters later, Jesus will show what it means to believe.)

John 7:37-39 "He that believeth on me, as the scripture hath said, out of his belly shall flow rivers of living water. This spake He of the Spirit which they that *believe* on Him *should receive*: for the Holy Ghost was not yet given ..." (emphasis added. They that believe should receive the Spirit, here identified as the Holy Ghost. Believing means more than mere mental assent that Jesus existed.)

2. The Gospel Commissioned

Mark 16:15-18 "Preach the gospel... He that believeth and is baptized shall be saved ..." (Not, he that believes and is saved should be baptized.) "These signs shall follow them that believe; in my name shall they cast out devils, they shall speak with new tongues, ... they shall lay hands on the sick, and they shall recover."

Luke 24:44-49 "Then opened he their understanding of the scriptures ... that repentance and remission of sins should be preached in his name ... tarry in Jerusalem until endued with power from on high." (We will have to go to the book of Acts to see if the apostles and disciples obeyed these commissions.)

Matthew 28:19 "Teach all nations, baptizing them in the name of the Father, and of the Son, and of the Holy Ghost." (What is the name? Note that "name" is singular, not plural. When we go to Part 3, The Gospel Preached, we will see how the apostles and disciples obeyed this Scripture, and we will clearly know what the "name" of the Father, and of the Son, and of the Holy Ghost is.)

Acts 1:1-3 "Jesus, through the Holy Ghost, gave commandments to the apostles … He showed himself alive by many infallible proofs, being seen of them forty days, and speaking of the things pertaining to the kingdom of God." ("Infallible proofs" in the Greek means "many criteria of certainty." I would love to spend forty days with Jesus. Here in the book of Acts we have the verbatim words of those who did. Don't you think they would know what He wanted them to preach?)

Acts 1:4-5, 8 "Wait for the promise … John baptized with water; but ye shall be baptized with the Holy Ghost not many days hence … ye shall receive power after the Holy Ghost is come upon you: and ye shall be witnesses …" (This was the last commission given just before Jesus ascended to heaven in verse 9. Jesus reminded them of John's message and told them they would be baptized with the Holy Ghost in a few days.)

Acts 1:9-15 "He was taken up … angels promised He will return in like manner. They returned to Jerusalem to an upper room to pray; about 120 disciples including Mary, mother of Jesus." (Some of the elements established in these commissions include: believing, repentance, baptizing, signs, healing, speaking with new tongues, and power to witness after being baptized with the Holy Ghost.)

3. The Gospel Preached

Acts 2:1-4 "They were all filled with the Holy Ghost and began to speak with other tongues as the Spirit gave them utterance." (This was the baptism of the Holy Ghost that was promised by Jesus a few days earlier in Acts 1:5.)

Acts 2:5-11 "This was noised abroad … how hear we every man in our own tongue wherein we were born?" (More than just the twelve apostles received the Holy Ghost because they were speaking in seventeen different languages. God made sure someone in the 120 was speaking in each language represented.) Acts 2:12-17 "These men are drunk. But Peter, standing with the eleven, began to preach ... This is that spoken by the prophet Joel ... in the last days, saith God, I will pour out of my Spirit upon all flesh ..." (Peter quoted the Old Testament prophet, Joel, Joel 2:28. Note: God's Spirit was to be poured out on "all flesh," not just the twelve apostles!)

Acts 2:36-42 "What shall we do?" (What will Peter, the man with the keys to the kingdom, preach? This is what we've been waiting to hear.) "Repent, and be baptized every one of you in the name of Jesus Christ for the remission of sins, and ye shall receive the gift of the Holy Ghost. The promise is to everyone God shall call. Save yourselves ... they that gladly received his word were baptized ... they continued steadfastly in the apostles' doctrine." (Now compare this with John 3:5, "born of water and of the Spirit," and Luke 24:47, "And that repentance and remission of sins should be preached in his name." Peter got it exactly right. This was the verbatim preaching of the apostle Peter telling us what to do to be saved. Is this an isolated case, or is there more?)

Acts 4:10-12 "By the name of Jesus Christ of Nazareth doth this man stand before you whole ... Neither is there salvation in any other: for there is none other name under heaven given among men, whereby we must be saved." (How does the name of Jesus save us? See Acts 2:38.)

Acts 10:1-6 "Cornelius was a devout man ... feared God ... gave much alms, prayed to God always." (He was a Gentile but probably more devout than many modern day Christians.) "He saw in a vision to send for Peter to tell him what he ought to do." (...to be saved, according to Acts 11:13-14. He was a good man, but goodness alone will not save.)

Acts 10:43-48 "While Peter spoke, the Holy Ghost fell on all them which heard the word ... the Jews were astonished that on the Gentiles also was poured out the gift of the Holy Ghost, for they heard them speak with tongues. Can any man forbid water that these should not be baptized?" (Wait, Peter, they have the Spirit, why worry about water baptism? Answer: John 3:5: "water and the Spirit.") "And he *commanded* them to be baptized in the name of the Lord." (Emphasis added.)

Acts 19:1-6 "Paul preached to disciples of John the Baptist … Have you received the Holy Ghost since you believed? John preached repentance and that they should believe on him which should come after … on Christ Jesus. When they heard this, they were baptized in the name of the Lord Jesus … the Holy Ghost came on them; and they spake with tongues …" (Paul rebaptized the disciples of John in the name of the Lord Jesus and they received the Holy Ghost and spoke with tongues, just as in Acts 2 and Acts 10. Are we picking up a pattern on the certainty of the gospel? In each case it was in obedience to John 3:5 and the commissions, by water baptism in the Name of Jesus, and receiving the Holy Ghost with the evidence of speaking with tongues!)

Acts 8:5-13 "Philip preached Christ at Samaria … saw miracles, demons cast out, healings, signs and there was great joy … they believed and were baptized, even Simon the sorcerer. (Were they saved? Nothing is said yet about the Holy Ghost. Some say it is automatic when you believe or are baptized, or have joy. We shall see.)

Acts 8:14-16 "The apostles sent Peter and John to pray for them to receive the Holy Ghost: For as yet he was fallen upon none of them: only they were baptized in the name of the Lord Jesus." (So, they didn't receive the Holy Ghost automatically when they were baptized, or when they had great joy. But how did they know they had not received the Holy Ghost yet? What evidence was lacking in their experience? They had been baptized in the name of the Lord Jesus, so why worry about the Spirit anyway? Answer: John 3:5: "water and the Spirit.")

Acts 8:17-21 "They laid their hands on them, and they received the Holy Ghost. When Simon saw that, he offered them money for this power …" (What did Simon see that would make him offer money? He was a sorcerer who had supernatural powers from Satan. He didn't offer money for the power to work miracles and signs in verse 13, but in verse 17, when they received the Holy Ghost, he saw an outstanding, miraculous experience that he had never seen before. In accordance with the pattern in Acts 2, 10, and 19, it was undoubtedly that they spoke with other tongues.)

It is a certainty that the gospel the apostles preached was: repentance, water baptism in the name of Jesus Christ for the remission of sins, and receiving the Holy Ghost with the evidence of speaking with tongues.

The apostles obeyed Matthew 28:19 by baptizing in the name of Jesus Christ. They understood that the "name" (singular) is Jesus. Father, Son, and Holy Ghost are not names, but titles, offices, or manifestations of the one true God. (I am a father, son, and husband, but I have only one name, and I'm not three persons.) Either the "name" in Matthew 28:19 is Jesus (see Acts 4:12) or the Scriptures contradict, the apostles were wrong, and we would have no confidence in anything they wrote. (For further study see John 14:7-11; John 14:16-18, 26; Colossians 2:9, and Isaiah 9:6.)

Baptism is Essential: John 3:5; Mark 16:16; Acts 2:38; Acts 8:16; Acts 10:48; Acts 19:5; I Peter 3:20-21

The Holy Ghost is Essential: John 3:5; John 7:38-39; Acts 2:1- 4, 38-39; Acts 8:17-18; Acts 10:45-46; Acts 19:6; Romans 8:9

Faith to Receive is Essential: John 7:38-39; Luke 11:9-13; Hebrews 11:6; Mark 11:24; Acts 2:4, 16-17, 38-39; Romans 10:17

The Word Will Prosper: Isaiah 55:9-12

THERE SHALL BE A PERFORMANCE

Wow! Did you hear the great news about Elisabeth being filled with the Holy Ghost? People have received the baptism of the Holy Ghost in many unusual places and diverse situations, e.g. on buses and trains, in restaurants, and even while receiving an offering at church ... but Elisabeth! This highly unusual incident would be hard to believe if not for the fact that it was fully documented in the Word of God: Elisabeth was miraculously filled with the Holy Ghost when her baby leaped in her womb! Both events stemmed from a surprise greeting from her cousin deep in the hill country of Judea: "And it came to pass, that, when Elisabeth heard the salutation of Mary, *the babe leaped in her womb*; and *Elisabeth was filled with the Holy Ghost* (Luke 1:41, emphasis added)! Elisabeth, the wife of Zacharias the priest, was six months with child (John the Baptist), when saluted by her cousin Mary, newly with child (Jesus Christ) "of the Holy Ghost," (Matthew 1:18).

This amazing alignment, a divinely orchestrated rendezvous of the "Voice" (Isaiah 40:3) and the "Lamb" (John 1:29), although thirty years premature, was bound to spark a divine intervention. The Spirit of the Lord evidently moved on John though he was just a babe in the womb. He surely sensed the preordained, prophetic urgency to introduce Jesus to the world as "the Lamb of God which taketh away the sin of the world" (John 1:29). But he was limited, by his warm and safe envelopment, to an anointed leap for joy: "... as soon as the voice of thy salutation sounded in mine ears, the babe leaped in my womb *for joy*" (Luke 1:44, emphasis added). Elisabeth was ultimately the surprised and happy beneficiary of this divine intervention.

John's Joyous Leap

It was more than just a little kick, it was a joyous leap, and it was contagious. Elisabeth instantly knew it was prompted by God, and she was immediately filled with an effusive, exuberant joy as she leapt her way into the kingdom of God! She was instantly saturated and immersed in the Holy Spirit of God, bursting forth in heavenly praise as the Spirit gave utterance! This was a preview of a future prophetic event: the birth of the Church on the Day of Pentecost (see Joel 2:28 and Acts 2:16-18). "And when the day of Pentecost was fully come, they were all with one accord in one place ... And suddenly there came a sound from heaven as of a rushing mighty wind, and it filled all the house where they were sitting ... And there appeared unto them cloven tongues like as of fire ... And they were all filled with the Holy Ghost, and began to speak with other tongues, as the Spirit gave them utterance" (Acts 2:1-4).

Elisabeth continued her supernatural utterance as, "... she spake out with a loud voice" (Luke 1:42), prophesying, "... Blessed art thou among women, and blessed is the fruit of thy womb. And whence is this to me, that the mother of my Lord should come to me? ... And blessed is she that believed: for *there shall be a performance of those things which were told her from the Lord.*" (Luke 1:42-45, emphasis added).

A Performance of What Things?

"Of those things which were told her from the Lord." (Luke 1:45). Namely: "... thou shalt conceive in thy womb, and bring forth a son, and shalt call his name JESUS. He shall be great, and shall be called the Son of the Highest: and the Lord God shall give unto him the throne of his father David: And he shall reign over the house of Jacob for ever; and of his kingdom there shall be no end" (Luke 1:31-33). The performance had already begun with Mary's miraculous conception and the childbirth that would follow. And the performance has continued to this day and will continue throughout all eternity.

"There Shall Be a Performance!"

This inspirational theme is prominent and recurrent throughout Scripture. After every promise He made, God could have inspired His writers to record: "There shall be a performance of what the

Lord told us!" And He often did, as we shall see in the following examples:

Paul exhorted the Philippian church: "Being confident of this very thing, that he which hath begun a good work in you will *perform* it until the day of Jesus Christ" (Philippians 1:6, emphasis added). And there was a performance!

Though Abraham and Sarah's bodies were dead to childbearing due to old age, they had a promise from God! Abraham "... staggered not at the promise of God through unbelief; but was strong in faith, giving glory to God; And being fully persuaded that, what he had promised, he was able also to *perform...*" (Romans 4:20-21, emphasis added). And there was a performance!

Jeremiah encouraged those carried away to Babylonian captivity: "For thus saith the LORD, That after seventy years be accomplished at Babylon I will visit you, and *perform* my good word toward you, in causing you to return to this place" (Jeremiah 29:10, emphasis added). And there was a performance!

God had earlier anointed Jeremiah, "Then said the LORD unto me, Thou hast well seen: for I will hasten my word to *perform* it" (Jeremiah 1:12, emphasis added). And there was a performance!

The apostle Paul knew beyond doubt that God would absolutely perform His promise, so he spread the good news to the weary, downcast, storm-tossed fellow sailors, "Wherefore, sirs, be of good cheer: for I believe God, that it shall be even as it was told me" (Acts 27:25). And there was a performance!

We can all find solace from the Psalmist David's 57th Psalm, as we take refuge under the shadow of His wings: "Be merciful unto me, O God, be merciful unto me: for my soul trusteth in thee: yea, in the shadow of thy wings will I make my refuge, until these calamities be overpast. I will cry unto God most high; unto God that *performeth* all things for me" (Psalm 57:1-2, emphasis added). And there was a performance!

Is there a take-away for us today from Elisabeth's miraculous infilling of the Holy Ghost and her anointed prophecy that followed? I believe there is. Perhaps we may be blessed to ....

Takhoma WORD!

> For the Lord himself shall descend from heaven with
> a shout, with the voice of the archangel, and with the
> trump of God: and the dead in Christ shall rise first:
> Then we which are alive and remain shall be caught
> up together with them in the clouds, to meet the Lord
> in the air: and so shall we ever be with the Lord.
>
> 1 Thessalonians 4:16-17

"There Shall Be a Performance!"

"Behold, I shew you a mystery; We shall not all sleep, but we shall all be changed, In a moment, in the twinkling of an eye, at the last trump: for the trumpet shall sound, and the dead shall be raised incorruptible, and we shall be changed" (1 Corinthians 15:51-52)!

"There Shall Be a Performance!"

"So when this corruptible shall have put on incorruption, and this mortal shall have put on immortality, then shall be brought to pass the saying that is written, Death is swallowed up in victory. O death, where is thy sting? O grave, where is thy victory?" (1 Corinthians 15:54-55)!

"There Shall Be a Performance!"

"And God shall wipe away all tears from their eyes; and there shall be no more death, neither sorrow, nor crying, neither shall there be any more pain: for the former things are passed away" (Revelation 21:4)!

"There Shall Be a Performance!"

How we do rejoice in knowing that God is both capable and faithful to perform all His exceeding great and precious promises, and that it is written: *"...there shall be a performance of those things which were told ... from the Lord"* (Luke 1:45 emphasis added).

Ron Schoolcraft

A CHRISTMAS STORY

I want to tell you a story about a young girl. This is a true story, and many of you around here will remember it. She was far from home, miles from her family, friends, and a warm bed. She had been on the road for several days, enduring the miserably cold weather. Her heart ached for her family, and her body ached for she was in considerable pain. She felt estranged from her family and friends. Under normal circumstances they would have been thrilled when she had told them she was expecting. But they were a very devout, conservative family and — well, she wasn't married. She had tried to explain — she was innocent, it wasn't like they thought. They just shook their heads. But what was worst of all, she had to tell the man she was engaged to — because he knew the child she was carrying obviously was not his! What a good man he was! Miracle of miracles! He *still* loved her; he *still* believed her story; *still* wanted to *marry* her!

Right now, she was in desperate need of another miracle, because he was walking toward her, after stopping at this hotel to get a room. It looked bad. With head down, he began shaking his head, "I'm so sorry, honey. No vacancy, they're completely filled up!" She burst into tears, "Joseph, what are we going to do? I'm in pain, I think the baby is almost ready to be born!" Joseph tried to comfort her, "It's going to be alright, Mary. The innkeeper is going to let us stay in his stable out back. It's kind of a cave where he shelters his cattle, sheep, and goats. It will give us some shelter. And guess what, Mary? The animal feeding trough — the manger —will make a perfect little cradle for our baby!"

So, this was how God came down to planet earth! The Almighty Creator of the Cosmos, Infinite in power, became a helpless little infant! Never in mankind's wildest imagination could we think the transcendent Creator of the Heavens, the earth, the sea, and all that in them is, would enter His earthly existence as a little Baby! But, yes, the Infinite became an Infant! Why not come as a massive shooting star, soaring out of the heavens, escorted by a hundred flaming angels on each side; circle the earth ten times, dropping lower each time around, trumpet sirens blaring, getting the attention of the whole world? Then gliding in like a chariot of fire, the Lord steps out in His shining apparel just like He wears in the Book of Revelation! NOT! He didn't come to glorify Himself; He came to seek and save the lost. Only God could have, would have, devised a plan to literally become one of us, so eventually we could be one with Him.

The Reason for the Taxing

Luke 2:1-5 "And it came to pass in those days, that there went out a decree from Caesar Augustus, that all the world should be taxed. (And this taxing was first made when Cyrenius was governor of Syria.) And all went to be taxed, every one into his own city. And Joseph also went up from Galilee, out of the city of Nazareth, into Judaea, unto the city of David, which is called Bethlehem; (because he was of the house and lineage of David:) To be taxed with Mary his espoused wife, being great with child."

I can only imagine: if I were Joseph, I would be protesting: "Wait just a minute! Lord, it's time for Mary to have her baby. There is absolutely no way she can make this trip bouncing all the way to Bethlehem on a donkey's back. Mary, what did that angel tell you? Did He say anything about Bethlehem? Did he say anything about taxing?! This is just not right!" Now just hold on Joseph! There's a reason for the taxing! *Messiah will be born in Bethlehem*! According to Micah 5:2, "But thou, Bethlehem Ephratah, though thou be little among the thousands of Judah, yet out of thee shall he come forth unto me that is to be ruler in Israel; whose goings forth have been from of old, from everlasting." Though Joseph and Mary couldn't see it, they would understand later. The taxing was needed to fulfill the prophecy of where Christ was to be born!

What about things that are taxing us today? Things that are vexing us, stressing us, trials, tribulations, Covid 19, social distancing, and broken hearts causing much anxiety. There is a reason! Romans 8:28 reveals, "All things work together for good to them that love God...." We may not find out all the good or even understand it completely, until much later. If for no other reason, it might be just to draw us closer to God, because we tend to seek God more when going through taxing times. And we are more blessed because of it. "Blessed is the man whom thou choosest and causest to approach unto thee" (Psalm 65:4).

Lightweight Trials Bring ....

Another reason for the taxing? "For our light affliction, which is but for a *moment, worketh for us* a far more exceeding and eternal weight of glory" (2 Corinthians 4:17, emphasis added). A trial doesn't feel "light" while you're going through it, but it is working for us, not against us!!! It is *working "for us* a far more exceeding and *eternal weight* of glory!" That's *heavy*! But the affliction is called "*light*." So, in summary:

Lightweight Temporary Trials Bring Heavyweight Eternal Blessings!

But I can imagine Joseph remaining unmollified. It seemed like everything that could go wrong, was going wrong. When the innkeeper sent them to the smelly stable full of animals, Joseph may have despaired: "If God is with us why is everything going against us? Mary, did the angel say anything about the baby being born in a smelly stable, in a cave? I just cannot believe God would allow this to happen to us!"

If any of our gentle readers have lived on a farm and ever been in a cattle barn, then you have smelled the pungent aroma that makes your eyes water. You will recall trying to breathe through your mouth, not your nose. And how it brought tears to your eyes. What really brings tears to my eyes, though, is when I think of how our Great Creator formed Adam from the dust of the ground and breathed into his nostrils the breath of life! How wonderful Adam's first breath must have been: the sweet, pure, fragrant air from the flowering fruit tree blossoms in the Garden of Eden! Not to mention that his lungs were inflated by God Himself as God breathed life into him! *But then* when the Infinite One became an infant Son and took His first breath of air on planet earth …. His delicate, pure little nostrils and lungs were singed, filled, and saturated with the stench of animal waste. This was how it began. He knew it would not be a picnic. Maybe He thought, so this is how it starts. Welcome to planet earth. Thirty-three years to Calvary. He was doing it all for us. He entered our world and became one of us, so we could be one with Him. "... who for the joy that was set before him endured the cross, despising the shame" (Hebrews 12:2).

****

The cattle were lowing, chewing their cud, eyelids drooping; a few lambs were bleating... Oh, what's this? Here comes a small group of bedraggled, breathless shepherds, eyes wide open with wonderment as they excitedly relate their amazing tale of an angelic choir praising God and of the angels' stunning announcement: "For unto you is born this day in the city of David a *Saviour, which is Christ the Lord.* And this shall be a sign unto you; Ye shall find the babe wrapped in swaddling clothes, lying in a manger" **(Luke 2:11-12,** emphasis added)! Huge smiles light their faces. They just can't stop looking at the Baby, trying to grasp how this Baby could be their Savior, Christ the Lord! They didn't even notice the odor.

Mary, Did You Know?

An awesome, award-winning song, "Mary Did You Know," was written about the birth and identity of Jesus Christ by Mark Lowry and Buddy Greene, in 1991. This song rapidly became a favorite at Christmas, as it dealt with the birth of Christ, revealing that this little Baby was, in reality, God manifest in the flesh (See 1 Timothy 3:16), by asking questions of His mother Mary. Here are some questions raised by the inspiring lyrics:

Mary, do you know your baby boy is the creator of the universe? Do you realize that He will someday rule the world? Do you understand He is heaven's perfect Lamb to be sacrificed for the sins of humankind? Do you know He is the Great I AM of Scripture? Do you understand your child will usher in a new era? Do you realize He will be your Savior, too? Do you recognize that when you kiss your baby's face, you are kissing God?

Yes, Mary Knew!

The Scripture abounds with clues to prove that Mary was well aware of the identity of her promised child:

> 1. Deuteronomy 6:4, "Hear, O Israel: The LORD our God is one LORD." This verse, the *Shema*, was memorized by all Jews, from their youth, and was the foundation of their monotheistic belief.

> 2. Luke 1:43 (emphasis added), "And whence is this to me, that the *mother of my Lord* should come to me?" Elisabeth, Mary's cousin and mother of John the Baptist, was filled with the Holy Ghost (Luke 1:41), and prophesied with a loud voice, proclaiming that Mary was the mother of her Lord! Mary knew clearly there was only one Lord!

> 3. Luke 1:46, 47 (emphasis added), "And Mary said, My soul doth magnify the *Lord*, And my spirit hath rejoiced in *God my Saviour*." Mary knew God was the Savior!

> 4. Luke 2:11 (emphasis added), "For unto you is born this day in the city of David a *Saviour*, which is *Christ the Lord*." The shepherds relayed this angelic declaration to Mary and Joseph. This was further confirmation to Mary that the Savior born, her baby, Jesus, was her Lord and her God!

> 5. Isaiah 7:14 (emphasis added), "Therefore the Lord himself shall give you a sign; Behold, a *virgin shall conceive*, and *bear a son*, and shall call his name *Immanuel*." Matthew 1:23 (emphasis added), "Behold, a virgin shall be with child, and shall bring forth a son, and they shall call his name *Emmanuel*, which being *interpreted is, God with us*." Mary's little baby was, clearly, *God with us*!

6. Matthew 1:21, "And she shall bring forth a son, and thou shalt call his name JESUS: for he shall save his people from their sins." The angel of the Lord gave this message to Joseph. He would certainly have told Mary! The name, JESUS, means "Jehovah-Savior" or "Jehovah is Salvation."

We could easily take the Christmas story for granted: the nativity scene, baby Jesus, the shepherds, etc. But we must not overlook this awesome truth: the Almighty God was made flesh! (John 1:1,14). He was born as a little baby! Can you imagine? The powerful, Almighty hand of God that flung the stars into space, and stretched forth the heavens, now, as the teeny, miniature hand of a newborn baby, reaches up and latches on to Mary's pinky finger! I can just see Joseph reach down and pick up baby Jesus, and there, safely nestled in the crook of the burly carpenter's arm, is: "THE MIGHTY GOD, THE EVERLASTING FATHER, THE PRINCE OF PEACE" (Isaiah 9:6, emphasis added)! **Yes, Mary knew!** And Joseph knew, too! And, glory to God in the highest, *we know also*!

Ron Schoolcraft

THOU Shalt Call His Name JESUS

The devout young Hebrew untied his work apron, shook it out, dusted himself off, and wiped the perspiration and sawdust from his brow. Then he brushed the wood chips and shavings from his hands and arms. He collapsed onto his workbench and, once again, as he often had the last few days, dropped into deep, troubled thought. The furrows in his forehead deepened as he continued rehearsing all the bizarre things that had happened to him. This incredible chain of events was so unbelievable that, try as he might, he could not get it out of his mind.

He faithfully attended the synagogue every sabbath and quoted the *Shema* every morning as he began his time of prayer: "Hear O Israel, the Lord our God is one Lord, and thou shalt love the Lord they God with all thine heart, and with all thy soul, and with all thy might" (Deuteronomy 6:4). He'd been trying to live a godly life, and loved studying the Law, the Psalms, and the Prophets. He felt so blessed because he did "not walk in the counsel of the ungodly, nor stand in the way of sinners, nor sit in the seat of the scornful" (Psalm 1:1). And he really knew he was blessed when, miracle of miracles, he was espoused to a beautiful, very devout Hebrew maiden. The smile spread across his face. That was the high point.

Well, he *thought* she was very devout. But how quickly it had all come crashing down: the heart-breaking news had crushed his very soul. No way, there was no way under the sun this horrible thing could be! She was not that kind of a girl. But now his beloved, his betrothed, was *expecting a child*! Oh, what a story she told. Something about an angel from God, telling her God's Spirit would overshadow her, and the baby would be Holy. How was I supposed to believe that? he thought. I wanted to ... but it was so far out of the realm of possibility. Nothing like this had ever happened before. But, then again, there was no way she could make up a story like that ... was there?

We tried so hard to keep this quiet. And did, except for my immediate family. They didn't believe her. But they believed me, they knew I was innocent. They insisted that I put her away, divorce her. They said, "By the law she should be stoned!" But I love her, and I say, "By love she should be forgiven and let live." They said, "If you don't divorce her, you'll go down in history as the foolish father of an illegitimate child. It will absolutely destroy your good reputation." So, I had made up my mind to divorce her, put her away, but privately, not publicly. I didn't want to ruin her reputation. (Or mine.)

Take Mary...

But then, would you believe, a ray of light — actually it was a roomful of dazzlingly bright light that shined down on me. I was shaking with fear, could hardly breathe. My family said it was some kind of a trance, a hallucination, or just something I ate! But I know it was an *angel*! I saw him! He spoke out loud to me, "Joseph, son of David, do not be afraid to *take Mary home as your wife*, because what is conceived in her is from the Holy Spirit. She will give birth to a son, and *you are to give him the name Jesus*, because he will save his people from their sins." (Matthew 1:20, 21, NIV, emphasis added).

Joseph looked over at Mary (she had been sitting there quietly the whole time); "The angel told me to marry you, Mary!" Mary nodded and smiled, "I know Joseph, you've told me many times. Please don't ever stop telling me that wonderful story." He smiled, "Mary, you're glowing! Speaking of angels ...."

Suddenly Joseph's countenance changed. The room grew darker. "But Bethlehem!" A candle flickered, almost went out. "The census, the taxes! We can't possibly make this journey, Mary. Your midwife said you're close. It's too dangerous to go through Samaria, so it will take at least a week with you bouncing on the back of a donkey all the way! Lord, why would you allow this to happen to us?" He shook his head. "There's just no reason, no earthly reason!" Mary pondered for a moment, then said softly, "Well, if there is no earthly reason, then there must be a *heavenly* one! I just believe God knows all about this. He will help us, Joseph. God is with us!"

Joseph nodded, "You're right, Mary. We need to be obedient. God is with us." Then he said, "You know Mary, I've been thinking … there's one thing I don't understand. You are so special; I can see why the Lord chose you to be the mother of Jesus. But me, I'm nothing. I'm just a nobody."

Mary frowned, "Oh, no, Joseph, don't you see? The Lord knew we were espoused. He chose *both* of us. The angel appeared to you also, so you are special! You are going to make the perfect Dad! You will raise him and train him in the fear and admonition of the Lord, in all the ways of the Lord! You will even teach him a trade, Joseph!"

Joseph said, "I will? Yes, I will! I'll teach him to be a carpenter!" He thought, then said, "But, you know what, Mary? I think He's going to train me and teach me the ways of the Lord. The name "Jesus" means "Jehovah-Savior," and "Jehovah is Salvation!" He's going to be … my Savior, my very Salvation! I think he'll be like a father to me!" Mary seemed stunned. "Joseph, you're right! And … to me also!"

Elisabeth's Revelation

Joseph said, "Mary, I've been wondering. What kind of a special child is this going to be? The angel told me that it was conceived of the Holy Spirit of God! And he told you the same thing, saying the 'power of the highest shall overshadow you'." Mary said, "Joseph, I haven't told you this yet. I've been pondering this for some time, and I think you should know. When I visited my cousin Elisabeth, she saluted me, and began speaking with a loud voice, like a prophetess! It was like the very oracle of God!" Joseph urged her, "What did she say?" Mary replied, "She said, 'Whence is this to me, that *the mother of my Lord* should come to me?' (Luke 1:43, emphasis added)" Joseph repeated, in awe, *"The mother of my Lord*! Mary! The *Shema* says there is only one Lord: 'Hear O Israel: the LORD our God is *One LORD*' (Deuteronomy 6:4, emphasis added). That means this little baby is...."

Joseph excitedly continued, "Mary, that's exactly what Isaiah said! It's all clear now! Speaking of the Messiah, he said, 'A virgin shall conceive and bear a son, and shall call his name Immanuel' (Isaiah 7:14). And we know Immanuel means, 'God with us!' Mary, baby Jesus is 'God with us'!" Mary nodded, tears filling her eyes.

Joseph cried, "Just a moment ago, Mary, we both said we could do this because we believed God is with us." He lowered his gaze, reached forth his hand, and gently touched her greatness. "He *really* is with us, Mary! He is '*God with us!*' Oh, Mary, I can't wait to see him!" Mary sobbed, "I can't wait to *hold Him!*"

Joseph, (now very excited), "We've got to get going! Stay right here, Mary! Stay calm! Don't go anywhere! I'm going out to saddle up our donkey. Bethlehem, here we come!"

He was gone just a few minutes, and burst back in, "Oh, Mary, I can't wait to see the luxurious place God has prepared for His birth. It's going to be like heaven, just out of this world!" Mary sighed, "I can only imagine."

****

And He Gave Him the Name Jesus!

So, did Joseph go down in history as the foolish father of an illegitimate son? Was his reputation ruined? Let's see what the Bible says: "When Joseph woke up, he did what the angel of the Lord had commanded him and took Mary home as his wife. But he did not consummate their marriage until she gave birth to a son. *And he gave him the name Jesus*" (Matthew 1:24-25, NIV, emphasis added)!

So, it was Joseph who officially gave Him the name, JESUS, at the rite of circumcision, just as the angel had instructed him to do! "She will give birth to a son, and *you are to give him the name Jesus*" (Matthew 1:21, NIV, emphasis added). Joseph was the first to call Him, Jesus! What a distinct and high honor. To be the first to introduce to the world that awesome Name of God which is above every Name, at which every knee shall bow, and every tongue confess (Philippians 2:9-11). "Neither is there salvation in any other: for there is none other name under heaven given among men, whereby we must be saved" (Acts 4:12)! It's the only saving name!

Joseph's ears were probably the first human ears to hear the name Jesus (from the angel), and his lips the first human lips to speak the name Jesus as he introduced the name of Jesus to the world! This was in keeping with the precedent set by Zacharias in naming John the Baptist following the angel Gabriel's instructions: "Thou shalt call his name John." At John's circumcision Zacharias wrote, "His name is John" (Luke 1:13, 63).

Joseph is rarely mentioned in the Bible after the birth of Jesus. We owe an overwhelmingly great debt of gratitude to this humble, unsung servant/hero, Joseph, who, without any fanfare or praise, raised Jesus in the fear, nurture, and admonition of the Lord. God has given me a much greater appreciation for this great man of God who introduced the matchless name of Jesus to the world. I want to meet him in heaven and thank him profusely! He should be easy to spot. Assuming Joseph gets a star in his crown for every time the name of Jesus saved, healed, blessed, or cast out demons, we can just go towards the glow. There may not be a large crowd around him. God willing, I'll be one of them. I expect I will see you there also.

The Blessings of a BHD (Broken Heart Degree)

Broken hearts come in all shapes and sizes and with varying degrees of intensity: from a "puppy love" grade school crush you had on someone that didn't know you existed (but it still hurt), to the devastating loss of a spouse, a child, parents, siblings, or other close family and friends, which causes our world to literally "turn upside down!" Other sources of broken hearts can be losing a job, bankruptcy, serious illness or injury, severe pain, infidelity, and divorce.

I'm sure most of us have experienced broken hearts (plural). We fall into three categories: past, present, and future: most of us have had broken hearts in the past, some of us have them right now, and probably all of us, sorry to say, will have more in the future. But the Bible clearly teaches there are blessings that come with brokenness, so let's look at some Scriptures and be encouraged. The news is not all bad. God Gave the Word to reveal the special blessings He has prepared to help us on our way.

Good Grief

Yes, grief can be "good," and broken hearts can bring blessings. The Bible tells us so:

Matthew 5:4 (emphasis added) "*Blessed* are they that *mourn*: for they shall be *comforted*." Mourning means a broken heart, and we *shall be*, not might be, comforted. And there is no comfort like God's comfort! "Blessed are ...")!

Psalm 30:5 "Weeping may endure for a night, but joy cometh in the morning." JOY! It is coming! It may be a long "night," a very long night, but if we endure hardness as a good soldier, we will start seeing the blessing of joy! Just how long, no one can say. Maybe one year, two years, several years; some say you will never get completely over it for, "Grief is the price of love, so great love brings great grief." But joy will still come. The sun will shine again!

Psalm 65:4 "Blessed is the man whom thou choosest, and causest to approach unto thee, that he may dwell in thy courts." Sometimes God allows broken hearts for a reason: He chooses us and causes us to approach, to draw closer to Him, to dwell in His courts! What a great blessing! At the same time, guess what else is happening? *He is drawing near to you* because of your broken heart!

Psalm 34:18 (emphasis added) "The LORD is *nigh* unto them that are of a *broken heart*; and saveth such as be of a contrite spirit." What a blessing! The Lord is NIGH! Further, Isaiah 55:6 declares, "Seek ye the LORD while he may be found, call ye upon him while he is *near*." And James 4:8 implores, "Draw nigh to God, and he will draw nigh to you." So, we get a head start: He is already nigh, because He is nigh to them with a broken heart! We are blessed with a Divine Conjunction, a Divine Alignment!

Psalm 147:3 "He healeth the broken in heart, and bindeth up their wounds." Healing and binding up are tremendous BLESSINGS!

Psalm 51:17 "The sacrifices of God are a broken spirit: a broken and a contrite heart, O God, thou wilt not despise." Others may not like your tears and brokenness, but they are sacrifices that God loves. He loves you, your broken spirit, and your broken and contrite heart, so you are BLESSED indeed!

Isaiah 57:15 (emphasis added) "For thus saith the high and lofty One that inhabiteth eternity, whose name *is* Holy; I dwell in the high and holy *place, with him also that is* of a *contrite and humble spirit*, to revive the spirit of the humble, and to *revive the heart of the contrite ones*." *He dwells with him also*! What an awesome BLESSING! He not only inhabits the praises of His people, but He *dwells with* the contrite, broken, and humble to revive their spirits and hearts! What abundant BLESSINGS!

Isaiah 61:3 (emphasis added) "To appoint unto them that *mourn* in Zion, to give unto them beauty for ashes, the oil of joy for *mourning*, the garment of praise for the spirit of heaviness." What tremendous blessings for those that mourn. Someone told me that grief would sometimes "ambush" me after I lost my beloved soulmate. I found it true, but the Lord showed me how to spring the ambush trap. He gave me: *"Turn your ambushes of grief into rendezvous of praise!"* I just began praising God for letting us meet, fall in love, get married, and for giving us three extraordinary daughters and their three cream-of-the-crop husbands, twelve awesome grands, eleven tremendous greats (and counting), and fifty-five glorious years together, etc! Though my tears continued flowing, they became tears of thanksgiving and praise! And my grief began subsiding! That is what this verse is saying: God gives "the oil of joy for mourning, the garment of praise for the spirit of heaviness."

Luke 7:22-23 (Emphasis added) (When John the Baptist, in prison, doubted Jesus and sent his disciples to question Jesus): "Then Jesus said, Go your way, and tell John what things ye have seen and heard; how that the blind see, the lame walk, the lepers are cleansed, the deaf hear, the dead are raised, to the poor the gospel is preached. And *blessed is he,* whosoever shall *not be offended in me."* Was John expecting Jesus to deliver him from prison? After all they were cousins! And he was the anointed forerunner, fulfilling Old Testament prophecy, who had introduced Jesus to the world. So what was John thinking as they led him to the chopping block? He was surely remembering Jesus last words for him: **"Blessed is he, whosoever shall not be offended in me."** He would not be delivered but would receive something greater: **he was BLESSED.** Luke 7:28 records, "For I say unto you, Among those that are born of women there is not a greater prophet than John the Baptist:" John was singularly **Blessed!** We must learn to pray, "I am not offended, Lord!"

Multiplied Blessings in Reading God's Word

There are so many comforting Scriptures, especially in Psalms! (See Solace from the Psalms). God will illuminate Scriptures you never noticed before because your needs are now different due to your broken heart! Be faithful to church, worship, and continue Bible reading and devotions! And God will pour out His promised blessings upon you!

Hebrews 4:15-16 "For we have not an high priest which cannot be touched with the feeling of our infirmities…Let us therefore come boldly unto the throne of grace, that we may obtain mercy, and find grace to help in time of need." He is touched by our broken hearts, so let us draw nigh, boldly, to *obtain mercy*, and *find grace*, such awesome blessings from God!

2 Corinthians 12:9 "And he said…My grace is sufficient for thee: for my strength is made perfect in weakness."

Psalm 77:10 (emphasis added) "And I said, This *is* my infirmity [anguish]: *but I will remember* the *years of the right hand of the most High*." Remember all those years and praise Him greatly for every one of them. Also, praise Him for every month, every week, and every day the right hand of the most High God blessed you! You will begin feeling abundantly *blessed* and grief must take a back seat!

Lamentations 3:22 "*It is of* the LORD'S mercies that we are not consumed, because his compassions fail not. *They are* new every morning: great *is* thy faithfulness." His wonderful compassion and faithfulness are invaluable *blessings*!

Romans 8:28 (emphasis added) "And we know that *all things work together for good* to them that love God, to them who are the called according to *his* purpose." We all know this phenomenal **blessing** is true although it may take a while to see it.

Isaiah 40:31 "But they that wait upon the LORD shall renew *their* strength; they shall mount up with wings as eagles; they shall run, and not be weary; *and* they shall walk, and not faint." Blessings!

Isaiah 41:10 "Fear thou not; for I *am* with thee: be not dismayed; for I *am* thy God: I will strengthen thee; yea I will help thee; yea I will uphold thee with the right hand of my righteousness." Note: here God *blesses* us with two great "*I Ams*," and three marvelous "*I wills*." BLESSINGS!

Psalm 91:1 "He that dwelleth in the secret place of the most High shall abide under the shadow of the Almighty." What glorious places in which to dwell and abide! Note: the "shadow of the Almighty" trumps "… the valley of the shadow of death," of Psalm 23:4!

Genesis 45:28 "And Israel said, *It is* enough; Joseph my son *is* yet alive: I will go and see him before I die." I felt sorry for Jacob: if he could have only known that Joseph was still alive, it would have spared him twenty years of grieving. Then it hit me! Our saved loved ones that have passed on are *still alive* in Paradise with Jesus! And "It is enough," for we shall "go and see them," (perhaps before we die!) At the rapture! (See 1 Thessalonians 4:16-18.)

Job 1:21 (emphasis added) "And [Job] said, … the LORD gave, and the LORD hath taken away; *blessed* be the name of the LORD." We should first focus on "the LORD *gave*." Oh, how He *gave*! If He had not first given them to us, we would have never had them. He took away to be with Him, because "Precious in the sight of the Lord is the death of his saints." (Psalm 116:15). He didn't take them away to hurt us, but to please Him and reward them. So, yes, we will say as Job, "*Blessed be the name of the Lord!*"

Philippians 3:10 (emphasis added) "That I may *know him*, and the power of his resurrection, and the *fellowship of his sufferings*, being made conformable unto his death;" His sufferings were not just physical pain. Isaiah 53:3 reveals, "He is despised and rejected of men; a man of *sorrows*, and acquainted with *grief*:" Consider this: when we are sorrowing and grieving with *broken hearts*, we are in *intimate fellowship with His sufferings*, and that will transition into a marvelous BLESSING!

Revelation 21:4 "And God shall wipe away all tears from their eyes; and there shall be no more death, neither sorrow, nor crying, neither shall there be any more pain: for the former things are passed away." This verse is a most comforting verse! But it wouldn't mean as much to us if we hadn't known Broken Hearts: tears, death, sorrow, crying, and pain!

Streams in the Desert, November 6. "My winter, and my tears, and weariness, Even my graves, may be His way to bless. I call them ills; yet that can surely be, Nothing but love that shows my Lord to me!"

Anne Voskamp (author of *1,000 Gifts*, *The Broken Way*, and *Be the Gift*), tells of her little girl, Shalom, cutting out a paper heart and trying to tape it to her chest. She accidentally ripped a big tear in it. Anne was waiting for her to cry, getting ready to console her. But Shalom said, "It's all Okay, Mama. Right here where the tear is, that's where the love of Jesus can get in, and come in and begin to heal it!" "Out of the mouth of babes ... thou hast perfected praise" (Matthew 21:16). Right where the break in your heart is will be the portal where He gains access to come in and draw nigh for healing and blessing you.

The Ultimate Blessing of a BHD

Bh.D. could also be the abbreviation for: *Doctor of Broken Hearts.* It was prophesied of our Lord: "He is despised and rejected of men; a man of *sorrows,* and acquainted with *grief* ... Surely he hath *borne our griefs*, and *carried our sorrows*" (Isaiah 53:3-4, emphasis added). He was scourged with the Roman cat-of-nine-tails and died alone at Calvary with a broken heart. Isaiah continued, "But he was wounded for our transgressions, he was bruised for our iniquities ... and with his stripes we are healed" (Isaiah 53:5). Thus, He became the ultimate, transcendent *Doctor of Broken Hearts*! The blessing for the Doctor is revealed in Hebrews 12:2: "... who for the **joy** that was set before him endured the cross, despising the shame..." It may not be too much to say that He was looking forward with great *joy and anticipation* to the *marriage supper of the Lamb to His Bride, the Church*, as recorded in Revelation 19:7-9. **This will be the ultimate blessing of the BHD, for both the Lamb and His Bride!**

Let us be thankful and praise God for the Blessings of our BHD!

THE BURDEN OF NEHEMIAH

Nehemiah is one of the lesser-known Old Testament Bible heroes compared to the likes of Moses, David, Joseph, Daniel, etc. Nevertheless, he ranks near the top in importance due to his far-reaching effect on important Bible prophecy. Although Nehemiah did not know it at the time, he served as the catalyst for a phenomenal prophetic event that is sometimes called the backbone of prophecy. Nehemiah's significant role is easily overlooked still today. Because of Nehemiah's burden we are beneficiaries of some absolutely amazing insights:

1) Nehemiah is linked to one of the most important prophetic passages in all of Scripture!

2) What Nehemiah does is linked to information on the Crucifixion of Christ, and the timing of it!

3) Nehemiah is linked to information on the antichrist and the tribulation period, and the exact length of it — seven years! All of this divine INTEL because of the Burden of Nehemiah!

In some ways he was a type of Christ. When his enemies tried to get him to come down off the wall that he was building around Jerusalem to meet with them, he said, "I'm doing a great work, I cannot come down!" (Nehemiah 6:3). This was a type of Christ on the Cross: "If thou be the Son of God, come down from the cross" (Matthew 27:40). Also, the enemy enticed Nehemiah, "Come, let us meet together ... in the plain of Ono. But they thought to do me mischief" (Nehemiah 6:2). In the plain of Ono? OH NO!

The southern kingdom of Judah was led into captivity in Babylon in 606 B.C. They began returning seventy years later in fulfillment of Jeremiah's prophecy (see Jeremiah 29:10) in three major expeditions: 1) Led by Zerubbabel, 536 B.C., they rebuilt the temple (see Ezra 1-6); 2) Led by Ezra, 458 B.C., he restored worship and led a revival of worship and the Word (see Ezra 7-10); and 3) Led by Nehemiah, 445-446 B.C., he rebuilt the walls of Jerusalem (see Nehemiah 1-13).

"I Wept, Mourned, Fasted and Prayed."

When Nehemiah heard about the condition of the walls around Jerusalem he became deeply burdened: "The wall of Jerusalem also is broken down, and the gates thereof are burned with fire. And it came to pass, when I heard these words, that I sat down and wept, and mourned certain days, and fasted, and prayed before the God of heaven..." (Nehemiah 1:3-4). Here again, Nehemiah was a type of Christ who also wept and prayed over Jerusalem. A spiritual parallel for us today is: how are the walls of our prayer life, Bible reading, fasting, faithfulness, outreach, witnessing, holiness, and separation? We must stay vigilant and keep our walls in good repair! "... because your adversary, the devil, as a roaring lion, walketh about, seeking whom he may devour" (1 Peter 5:8). The devil will try to breech the walls.

Nehemiah continued: "O Lord, I beseech thee, let now thine ear be attentive to the prayer of thy servant, and to the prayer of thy servants, who desire to fear thy name: and prosper, I pray thee, thy servant this day, and grant him mercy in the sight of this man. For I was the king's cupbearer" (Nehemiah 1:11). As the king's cupbearer he had a position of great importance and influence. Also, one of high trust and responsibility. But he risked his life daily by drinking of the king's beverages to see if they were poison in order to thwart any assassination attempt and to save the king's life!

In chapter 2, Nehemiah became so burdened that the king recognized his sadness. Nehemiah became "very sore afraid" (Nehemiah 2:2). Why? Because to appear sad in the presence of the king was an unpardonable sin, punishable by death! Nehemiah made his request: "And I said unto the king, If it please the king, and if thy servant have found favour in thy sight, that thou wouldest send me unto Judah, unto the city of my fathers' sepulchres, that I may build it" (Nehemiah 2:5).

God's Timeclock Starts Ticking!

"And the king said unto me, (the queen also sitting by him,) For how long shall thy journey be? and when wilt thou return? So *it pleased the king to send me*; and I set him a time" (Nehemiah 2:6, emphasis added)! Put a star by this verse! This is the LINK! As we shall see in Daniel 9, this verse started God's timeclock ticking on one of the most important prophecies of the Bible — **Daniel's Seventy Weeks!**

Note the highly unusual reference: "(the queen also sitting by him)!" You know who this queen is. She is undoubtedly Queen Esther! Some Bible scholars believe her husband, Ahasuerus, was the same as Artaxerxes (others say Artaxerxes was her son or stepson). Now we know why he was so kind to the Jews! And to Nehemiah! Perhaps Esther could still hear Mordecai saying, "who knoweth whether thou art come to the kingdom for such a time as this?" (Esther 4:14). Here Nehemiah was also a type of Moses, when he "refused to be called the son of Pharaoh's daughter; Choosing rather to suffer affliction with the people of God, than to enjoy the pleasures of sin for a season" (Hebrews 11:24-25).

Nehemiah wisely asked the King to commission, authorize, and supply him. "And the king granted me, according to the good hand of my God upon me" (Nehemiah 2:8). He then encouraged them, "Come, let us build up the wall of Jerusalem," and reminded them, "Then I told them of the hand of my God which was good upon me ... And they said, Let us rise up and build. So they strengthened their hands for this good work" (Nehemiah 2:17-18).

In chapter 3, Nehemiah divided the work among forty-two groups, all united, all along the wall with no separation, as laborers together. Each had a portion, and many built "over against his house ... his chamber." (see verses 10, 23, 28, 29 and 30). Many whose homes were near the wall, would make sure they built it right. Proving once again that it all begins at home. Our serving God also begins at home! It has often been said that a church is no stronger than its homes and families. We must build a wall of family togetherness, through prayer, Bible reading, and attending church together.

Ron Schoolcraft

Daniel's Seventy Weeks

In Daniel chapter nine, the angel Gabriel appeared to the prophet Daniel in a vision: "Yea, whiles I was speaking in prayer, even the man Gabriel, whom I had seen in the vision at the beginning, being caused to fly swiftly, touched me about the time of the evening oblation. And he informed me, and talked with me, and said, O Daniel, I am now come forth to give thee skill and understanding. At the beginning of thy supplications the commandment came forth, and I am come to shew thee; for thou art greatly beloved: therefore understand the matter, and consider the vision" (Daniel 9:21-23).

Gabriel opened Daniel's understanding: "*Seventy weeks* are determined upon thy people and upon thy holy city, to finish the transgression, and to make an end of sins, and to make reconciliation for iniquity, and to bring in everlasting righteousness, and to seal up the vision and prophecy, and to anoint the most Holy" (Daniel 9:24, emphasis added). Note the phrase: "seventy weeks." The Hebrew word for "weeks" means "sevens." So, are these "sevens" seven-*day* periods or seven-*year* periods? We see from the context that they are seventy, *seven-year* periods, totaling four-hundred ninety years. "... to make an end to sins...bring in everlasting righteousness...and to anoint the most Holy." This is clearly a vision about the end of time and the beginning of eternity.

"Know therefore and understand, that *from the going forth of the commandment to restore and to build Jerusalem ...*" (Daniel 9:25, emphasis added). This is the LINK clearly referring to Nehemiah 2:6, when King Artaxerxes commissioned Nehemiah to go to Jerusalem to rebuild the walls and the city! This started God's clock ticking on Daniel's seventy weeks! From that commandment, "... unto the Messiah the Prince shall be seven weeks and threescore and two weeks..." (Daniel 9:25 continued), thus, totaling sixty-nine weeks. Breaking it down: seven weeks (forty-nine years) to rebuild the streets and walls of Jerusalem; "And after sixty-two weeks, [four-hundred thirty-four years], shall Messiah be cut off [Jesus crucified!]" (Daniel 9:26). This totals four-hundred eighty-three years.

There is much evidence for using a calendar year of three-hundred sixty days instead of three-hundred sixty-five days. (The earlier calendar year was twelve months of thirty days each.) Then the four-hundred eighty-three years would calculate to be only four-hundred seventy-six years. If the command to rebuild the walls were 446 B.C., then, subtracting four-hundred forty-six from four-hundred seventy-six, Jesus would have been crucified in A.D. 30, between thirty-three and thirty-four years of age. Many Bible scholars currently believe that Jesus was born in 4 B.C or earlier.

The Missing 70th Week?

But the seven weeks and sixty-two weeks total only sixty-nine weeks! God's clock stopped ticking when Messiah was cutoff (crucified) at the end of the 69th week. What happened to the missing final week of Daniel's Seventy Weeks? Verse 27 has the answer!

"And he ["the prince that shall come" of the preceding verse, Daniel 9:26] shall confirm the covenant with many for *one week...*" (Daniel 9:27, emphasis added). This will be for seven years, because each week is seven years, not seven days. So, here is the 70th week of Daniel's Prophecy and it will start the clock ticking again on Daniel's Seventy Weeks! When the antichrist negotiates a major peace treaty between the Jews and the surrounding Arab nations, solving the long-standing middle east crisis, this will start the seven-year tribulation period!

BUT "... in the *midst of the week* he shall cause the sacrifice and the oblation to cease, and for the overspreading of *abominations* he shall make it *desolate*, even until the consummation, and that determined shall be poured upon the *desolate*" (Daniel 9:27 continued, emphasis added). The antichrist, after three and a half years (in the "midst of the week" of seven years) will claim to be God, break the treaty and set up his own image in the temple: "Who opposeth and exalteth himself above all that is called God, or that is worshipped; so that he as God sitteth in the temple of God, shewing himself that he is God" (2 Thessalonians 2:4). This begins the "abomination of desolation" spoken of by Jesus: "But when ye shall see the abomination of desolation, spoken of by Daniel the prophet, standing where it ought not..." (Mark 13:14).

All of this prophetic endtime INTEL, is one of the strongest evidences of the supernatural inspiration of the Scripture! And it's all because Nehemiah had a burden, and wept, mourned, fasted, prayed, petitioned the king, and gave himself to God!

It is obvious that both my pastor Larry Arrowood, and pastor-elect Aaron Arrowood, along with many more pastors are under a burden to win souls and have a great revival and an outpouring of the Holy Spirit. May God help us all to get a burden like Nehemiah. Let's ask God for a burden for our CHURCH, our CITY, and our NATION!

"This know also, that in the last days perilous times shall come" (2 Timothy 3:1). If times do get perilous, may God send the lost to us, especially a lot of backsliders that see the signs of the times! May God make us a glorious church for perilous times!

PART V

POEMS AND SONGS

Who his own self bare our sins in his own body on ...

1 Peter 2:24

The Tree

I think that I shall never see
A poem lovely as The Tree.

The Tree that looked for God all day,
Then found it held Him in its sway.

The Tree that felt it lacked the worth
To lift the Savior from the earth;

Yet dared to raise the BRANCH on high,
Emboldened by the WORD so nigh.

The Tree that did in sorrow wear
A nest of thorns placed cruelly there;

Upon whose boughs the Lamb was pressed
By love from His sweet flowing breast.

Upon whose bosom, Precious Stain
Of crimson blush, the Lamb was slain!

Ron Schoolcraft

The Tree of death, the prophet said,

Thereby did crush the serpent's head.

Unveiled — it stands — today!

The Tree of Life!

LIFE for you and me!

With sincere appreciation to Joyce Kilmer (1886-1918) whose classic poem "Trees" served as the model.

This song may be viewed as a music video on the author's YouTube channel: creatorwise   My daughter, Julia, composed the music and produced the video, including graphics, instrumentation, and vocals in 2021. May "The Tree," as a personification of the Cross of Christ, give us a deeper appreciation of the supreme sacrifice our great Creator paid to become our Savior.

THE BACK SIDE OF CALVARY

When you find yourself at Calvary with Jesus crucified,

Crawl behind the Cross please, take a look at the back side,

And there behold His stripes, and with tears realize ....

He's got *your* back, but He gave *His* ... to the smiter.

Chorus

God gave His back to the smiter, then died at Calvary;

His stripes bought your healing, His death set you free.

He's still the All-time World Champion, Undefeated Fighter,

And He's got *your* back, all because He gave *His* to the smiter.

Well, Satan thought he had Him beaten, thought he had the upper hand

Till the Victim became the VICTOR! It was all part of God's Plan.

So, "Satan get behind me!" With victory declare.

God's got your back and Satan knows he doesn't have a prayer.

Bridge

Of so many stripes for you and for me,

But each cutting lash bought countless victories!

By those stripes we're healed, at Calvary redeemed!

That's why I love you Jesus ... You did it all for me ... for me!

End: You could have saved yourself, but you saved me ...

"I gave my back to the smiters..." (Isaiah 50:6).

Ron Schoolcraft

This song may be viewed as a music video on Julia's YouTube music channel: Dawns Harvest. Julia composed the music and produced the video, including graphics, instrumentation, and vocals, with an assist from Rhonda Bowling on the vocals.

THE THIEF AND THE CHRIST

Such screamin' and such cursin' I never thought I'd hear;
Such profane oaths and wicked words, not fit for "holy" ears.
But those priests just stand there grinnin' as if they're havin' fun,
While three men suffer on a cross; oh, why must I be one!

I know that I'm a sinner, this I can't deny,
And my buddy hangin' yonder there, we both deserve to die;
But this battered man between with bloody back and crimson brow,
Why did they crucify Him? He was half dead anyhow.

Now Pilate's sign, "King of the Jews," is nailed where all can see.
The high priest screams, "If you're God's Son then come down off that tree!"
Such taunts and accusations, my ears have never heard.
The thing that bothers me, that man has never said a word.

I've heard a lot about Him, this man from Galilee;
He haled blind eyes and lepers, set captive spirits free.
Even as they mock Him now His love comes shinin' through;
He prays, "Forgive them Father, for they know not what they do."

These cramps and spasms wrack my tortured body constantly;
A thousand knives rip through me as I writhe in agony.
I shouldn't cry, compared to Him I still look like a man.
The last time I saw that much blood? The Passover Lamb.

The sky is getting darker now, black clouds rollin' in;

Surely it can't be --- does nature sympathize with Him?

There's something goin' on here, somehow I don't quite see;

What is this God-man doin' hangin' on this cursed tree?

My buddy joins that insane mob with shouts of mockery,

But I cry, "When your Kingdom comes, Lord, please remember me!"

Though pain still roars, my spirit soars, as love shines through His eyes,

And He softly says, "This day you'll be with me in Paradise."

His mother and disciples weep in sorrow and despair.

Did they not hear Him promise me that Paradise so fair?

They're actin' like they think that this must surely be the end;

Am I the only one who knows? This King will live again!

I know He could come down from here if He really wanted to.

Oh people, can't you see? Somehow, He's doin' this for you!

Someday they'll surely understand, someday they'll surely see,

The truth that He was crucified for His Bride-to-be!

Yes, now I know if He does die, it will not be in vain;

He surely has a plan in mind for those who trust His Name.

Oh, come on death, I'm ready now. Ha! Where is your sting?

I'm not afraid to die now, I've been pardoned by the King!

GOD GAVE THE WORD

Chorus

I believe, I believe, I believe I have been pardoned by Jesus Christ my King!

I believe, I believe, I believe that I shall live again with Jesus Christ my King!

I believe, I believe, I believe I have been pardoned by Jesus Christ my King!

I believe, I believe, I believe that I shall live again with Jesus Christ my King!

Ron Schoolcraft

The Carpenter of Calvary

With sawdust-sprinkled hands and arms and woodchip-frosted hair,
And a fragrant smell of rough-hewn cedar wafting through the air,
The Carpenter from Nazareth in backwoods Galilee,
Dreamed of how His greatest work of art was soon to be.

He'd formed the worlds and framed them with the hammer of His
WORD;
Now tabernacled in the flesh, He was the Carpenter.
The One who measured out the seas and heavens with the span,
Now knew the plan to save mankind lay in His chiseled hands.

Then a splinter pierced His finger, and the crimson slowly traced
Along the beam of time until a shadow crossed His face.
"Now son, that didn't hurt that bad," Dad sponged away the stain.
"You're gonna be a carpenter, acquaint yourself with pain."

The Master Builder knew the cost for a building fitly framed,
And trembled as He gently smoothed His hand across the grain.
He longed to labor with His hands, to tarry longer still,
But time was up: He had to move His workshop to the Hill.

Upon that Hill the Carpenter bowed low beneath the strain,
And toiling there in silence, wrought with blood and sweat and pain;
And once again He stretched His hands to build a new creation,
And took the nails in deep travail of driven desperation.

GOD GAVE THE WORD

At last, He cried, "It's finished!" His Masterpiece was through.

Many were astonished at the visage now in view:

For there was LOVE! with arms spread wide, uplifted from the earth;

The Carpenter, at Calvary, unveiled His Crowning Work!

Chorus

Oh_____ Carpenter of Calvary, You labored in great pain upon that tree;

And when your work was done, unveiled to everyone, your Masterpiece of Calvary!

Ron Schoolcraft

THE HIDING PLACE

Last night I heard my children play a game called hide-and-seek;

As they rushed to hide my little girl tried so hard not to peek.

Then to my surprise tears filled my eyes as they played on happily,

For in a children's game the Spirit came, somehow to speak to me.

Chorus I

"Here I come, ready or not," it seems I heard the Savior say.

"Time's up, my child, I can no longer wait.

If your hiding place is in my grace, I'll find you right away,

In a moment — in a twinkling — I'll take you home to stay."

I thrilled to watch a bride preparing for her wedding day;

Such a pretty sight in spotless white, adorned in fine array.

Then my heart rejoiced to hear God's voice as He spoke to me once more,

And said, "My bride, I'm just outside, now reaching for the door."

Chorus II

"Here I come, ready or not," it seems I heard the Bridegroom say.

"Time's up, my bride, I can no longer wait.

If your hiding place is in my grace, I'll find you right away,

In a moment — in a twinkling — I'll take you home to stay."

"Take heed that none deceive you for my coming is at hand.

Though sin abounds, my grace surrounds you now to help you stand,

Till I choose a day — just like today — to take my church away;

It won't be long, you're almost home, forevermore to stay."

This song may be viewed as a music video on the author's YouTube channel: creatorwise   Music/Vocals: author's family; Video/Graphics: Jaredith Mize; Audio Engineer: Larry Spall; Bass Guitar: Kevin Bowling; Drums: Seth Spall

Ron Schoolcraft

The Sacrifice of Praise

Let us offer the sacrifice of praise to God continually,

That is, the fruit of our lips giving thanks to his name.

Hebrews 13:15

With my heart bowed low and my hands upraised,

I offer you, God, my continual praise:

The fruit of my lips, giving thanks to your Name;

The fruit of my eyes, through my tears unashamed;

The fruit of my heart, even though it is broken.

It swells with your love and your joy unspoken;

It's filled with your peace, past all understanding,

And compassionate love that is ever expanding.

Please enlarge my heart that it might contain more

To delight in you for, than ever before;

And when you grant my desires, as you promised to do,

My chief desire is — to delight more in you!

"Delight thyself in the Lord; and he shall give thee the desires of thine heart" (Psalm 37:4).

And one more thing Lord: I'm so grateful to you,

For turning grief's ambush to a praise rendezvous!

©2019 Ron Schoolcraft

The Smell of Your Sunburnt Skin

(Childhood Memories with Our Awesome Daughters: Rhonda, Angela & Julia)

I fondly remember our bedtime rites, when I climbed up to tuck you in;

But you sent me back down, "Please, a winter drink, Daddy," you begged with an impish grin.

Then, "Rock-a-Bye-Baby," with pillow-squeezed ears, you gave me a sweet toothless grin.

But I guess the thing I remember the most was the smell of your sunburnt skin.

Oh, how the wind blew and that cradle did rock! Oh, no, it fell free from the limb!

"Then down will come (Rhonda/Angie/Julie) cradle and all!" You cried, "Daddy, do it again!"

You squealed with delight as I rocked you once more; you relive it now says your grin!

Yet through it all what I fondly recall was the smell of your sunburnt skin.

Just when I think those days are long gone, and I'll never see them again,

Your children yell, "Granna can we stay all night?" Yep, we've come full circle, and then ...

I notice the reek of the grime and the dirt, but what fills my face with a grin,

And my heart with joy and my eyes with tears .... is the smell of *their* sunburnt skin!

© 2018 Ron Schoolcraft

Ron Schoolcraft

Our Pioneers of Faith

A Tribute to my Father-in-Law, Rev. Grover J. Myers

March 13, 1916 — November 1, 2004

As we reflect on bygone days and battles we have won,

Let's not forget our pioneers and how they first begun.

We call them pioneers of faith, for faith was all they had;

But faith was all they needed when things around looked bad.

Though "things around" looked bad a lot, that didn't slow them down;

They fought the devil hand to hand and kept on gaining ground.

And that ground they fought so dearly for, we stand on here today,

And the gospel road we cruise along — yes, they paved the way.

Those Pentecostal pioneers — they proudly blazed the trail;

It was for us they put their trust in Him who would not fail.

They didn't have a fancy church; good music — it was rare,

But with their fasting, prayer, and praise, God's glory filled the air.

They preached the coming of the Lord with great anticipation;

If not for them, we wouldn't be the rapture generation.

So, in our hearts we find for them a very special place;

With love and honor, we salute — our pioneers of faith.

© 1981 Ron Schoolcraft

My Lovely Marcella

A Tribute to My Proverbs 31 Wife

My lovely Marcella, the girl who excellest them all;
In the midst of the darkness my virtuous woman stands tall;
Her price is far greater than rubies and diamonds and all;
My lovely Marcella, the girl who excellest them all.

She maketh fine linen and willingly works with her hands;
Her husband is known in the gates with the men of the land;
She will do him good for in her is no evil, at all;
My lovely Marcella, the girl who excellest them all.

She opens her mouth with wisdom and kindness and grace;
Her husband and children will rise up and sing of her praise;
She stretches her hand to the poor of the land, young and old;
My lovely Marcella, the girl who's more precious than gold.

She layeth her hands to the tapestried fabric of life;
Honor and strength are the clothing of my virtuous wife;
When her family needs her, she faithfully answers the call;
Of the many fair daughters, my Marcella excels them all.

A virtuous woman, oh where can we find one today?
The heart of her husband will trust in her safely always;
Now, I must confess that I have been blessed, above all;
With lovely Marcella, the girl who excellest them all.

© 1988 Ron Schoolcraft

Endnotes

1. Henry Morris, PhD, Father of modern creation science movement, founder of Institute for Creation Research

2. Matthew Henry, ⌈⌈ Hendrickson Academic; Unabridged edition (June 9, 2009) Hendrickson Academic; Unabridged edition (June 9, 2009)

3. jumpintotheWord.com, 20 interesting facts about the Bible, May 5, 2015

4. Fred Hoyle, The Intellegent Universe, ⌈Holt Rinehart & Winston; First Edition (January 1, 1983)

5. Rosenberg, Marc. October 10, 2017. Marc My Words: The Coming Knowledge Tsunami. Learning Solutions. Accessed   April 14, 2021.

6. THE LIFE MILLENNIUM (New York, NY: LIFE BOOKS Time Inc., 1998) 169

7. Henry Morris, Men of Science Men of God (El Cajon, CA: Master Books, 1988) 23-26

8. THE LIFE MILLENNIUM (New York, NY: LIFE BOOKS Time Inc., 1998) 169

9. ibid, 175

10. ibid, 176

11. Henry Morris, Men of Science Men of God (El Cajon, CA: Master Books, 1988) 37

12. ibid, 85

13. Josh McDowell, MORE evidence that demands a verdict (Campus Crusade for Christ, 1975), 322

14. Lee Strobel, The Case for Christianity Answer Book (Nook Ed.), (Grand Rapids, MI: Zondervan, 2014) 57

15. ibid, 60

16. https://crossexamined.org/voltaires-prediction-home-and-the-bible-society-truth-or-myth-further-evidence-of-verification/

17. Rosenberg, Marc. October 10, 2017. Marc My Words: The Coming Knowledge Tsunami. Learning Solutions. Accessed April 14, 2021.

18. George S. Patton, Jr., War As I Knew It, (New York, NY: Bantam Books, 1980) 320,321,385

19. ibid, 320, 382

20. ibid, 335

21. Max Lucado (January 11, 1955), a former missionary, international speaker, American author of multiple books, and minister at Oak Hills Church in San Antonia, TX.

22. Lewis, C.S., Mere Christianity, (New York: the Macmillan Company, 1952), 40-4 Ibid, 40, 41

23. ibid, 40,41

24. McDowell, Josh, Evidence That Demands a Verdict, (Campus Crusade for Christ, 1972), 107-112

25. William E. Booth-Clibborn, Down From His Glory, © 1921

26. New trends in evolutionary biology: biological, philosophical and social science perspectives. November 2016 scientific meeting. The Royal Society: Posted on royalsociety.org, accessed April 20, 2021.

27. Hands, J. Is it time to drop Darwinism? Science Focus. Posted on sciencefocus.com November 22, 2016, accessed April 17, 2021.

28. MacAllister, J. Environmental evolution: effects of the origin and evolution of life on earth newsletter. Posted on Envevo.org January 2017, accessed April 16, 2021.

29. Marshall, P. Royal Society's "New Trends in Biological Evolution" -- A Bloodless Revolution. Evolution2. Posted on evo2.org November 30, 2016, accessed April 16, 2021.

30. Charles Darwin, Origin of Species, 6th ed., Ch. 10, para. 1.

31. Luther Sunderland, Darwin's Enigma: Fossils and Other Problems, (El Cajon, CA: Master Books, 1988).

32. Colin Patterson, personal communication; documented in Luther Sunderland, Darwin's Enigma: Fossils and Other Problems, (El Cajon, CA: Master Books 1988) 88-90.

33. D.M. Raup and J.M. Stanley, Principles of Paleontology (San Francisco: W.H. Freeman and Co., 1971) 306

34. S.J. Gould, Natural History, 86(S):13 (1977).

35. Stephen C. Meyer, Return of the GOD Hypothesis, (New York, NY: HarperOne, 2021)

36. Fred Hoyle, "The Universe: Past and Present Reflections" Engineering & Science, November, 1981, 8-12

37. Stephen C. Meyer, Signature in the Cell, (New York, NY: HarperOne, 2009)

38. Lee Strobel, The Case for a Creator (Grand Rapids, MI: Zondervan, 2004) 204-206

39. ibid, 281-282

40. ibid

41. Stephen C. Meyer, Return of the GOD Hypothesis, (New York, NY: HarperOne, 2021) 173

42. Lee Strobel, The Case for a Creator (Grand Rapids, MI: Zondervan, 2004) 225

43. ibid, 221

44. ibid, 244, 282

45. Francis Collins, "My Journey from Atheism to Christianity" YouTube, Veritas Forum, Francis Collins at Caltech, accessed December 22, 2023

46. Immanuel Kant, Critique of Practical Reason, (1788).

47. Lee Strobel, The Case for Christianity Answer Book (Nook Ed.), (Grand Rapids, MI: Zondervan, 2014) 129

48. David Bernard, Anchor Points (Weldon Spring, MO: Word Aflame, 2022) 113

49. Lee Strobel, The Case for Christianity Answer Book (Nook Ed.), (Grand Rapids, MI: Zondervan, 2014) 31-33

50. Lee Strobel, The Case for Christianity Answer Book (Nook Ed.), (Grand Rapids, MI: Zondervan, 2014) 31-33

51. Henry M. Morris, The Henry Morris Study Bible (Green Forest, AR: Master Books, 2017) 1399

52. Jenny Lee Riddle, Revelation Song, © 2009

53. William E. Booth-Clibborn, Down From His Glory, © 1921

54. Henry Morris, The New Defender's Study Bible (Nashville, TN: World Publishing, Inc, 2006) 843

55. ibid, 1626

www.ingramcontent.com/pod-product-compliance
Lightning Source LLC
LaVergne TN
LVHW051230080426
835513LV00016B/1511

* 9 7 8 1 9 6 1 4 8 2 1 3 5 *